THE FRANCHISING WAY

Go International, Expand Your Network, and Sell Just About Anything

KAREN KWAN

PARTRIDGE

Copyright © 2019 by Karen Kwan.

ISBN:	Hardcover	978-1-5437-4950-2
	Softcover	978-1-5437-4949-6
	eBook	978-1-5437-4951-9

All rights reserved. No part of this book may be used or reproduced by any means, graphic, electronic, or mechanical, including photocopying, recording, taping or by any information storage retrieval system without the written permission of the author except in the case of brief quotations embodied in critical articles and reviews.

Because of the dynamic nature of the Internet, any web addresses or links contained in this book may have changed since publication and may no longer be valid. The views expressed in this work are solely those of the author and do not necessarily reflect the views of the publisher, and the publisher hereby disclaims any responsibility for them.

Print information available on the last page.

To order additional copies of this book, contact
Toll Free 800 101 2657 (Singapore)
Toll Free 1 800 81 7340 (Malaysia)
orders.singapore@partridgepublishing.com

www.partridgepublishing.com/singapore

Contents

Preface vii

Preface ix

Chapter 1   Introduction to Franchising 1

Chapter 2   Have Power of International Brand.................................... 14

Chapter 3   Assess the Franchising Suitability for Your Business 25

Chapter 4   Package Your Concept Uniquely for Franchising.............. 36

Chapter 5   Build a Franchise Revenue Plan...48

Chapter 6   Learn the Seven Key Elements to a Replicable Franchise System 62

Chapter 7   Learn from the International Franchise Winners 81

Chapter 8   Franchise Law in Hong Kong.. 91

Chapter 9   Franchise System Development Time Schedule and Financial Investment...99

Chapter 10 Go International... 108

Preface

Karen is a good friend of mine for many years. Together, we have established the Asia Branding and Franchising Association. Through the operation and development of the association, we hope to influence more entrepreneurs to focus on brand development and understand the franchise business so as to grow their business successfully! When I work with Karen, what she impressed me most was her thorough analysis and enthusiasm for the franchise business in addition to clear business thinking.

Karen's new book is about to be published recently. This is actually a bible for entrepreneurs. After reading this book, you will learn how to be start your business even in a period of short of funds, lack of core team and business model. Under the guidance of some successful commercial cases, this book teaches you how to set up a simple and replicable franchise system, how to deliver your products and services to end-users and how to double your sales performances so as to improve the cash flow.

As the founder of the B.Duck brand, I am honored to read the book and write a preface for Karen. During the development of my career and brand for more than a decade, I have encountered many difficulties. I believe the development of B.Duck would go further successful if I have read this book ever before starting my business!

I sincerely recommend to those who are interested in starting a business and want to understand the franchising system. I am sure you will be inspired by the successful entrepreneurs and get mastered of being different from the market practise!

Eddie Hui

Semk Products (Holdings) Limited

Managing Director & CEO

Preface

Franchising is one of business models to grow your business in any market. I have studied and expanded the business internationally through franchising in past few years, but I cannot find much Chinese books about franchising. I am excited when Karen passes me the manuscript of this book. This book covers solid foundational knowledge about franchising with support of real-life case studies. In addition, it provided detailed practical advices on evaluating and developing your franchising business. This book is good for both business owners who wants to understand more about franchising and business executives who have the responsibility to implement franchising. Appreciate much Karen's dedicated effort to contributing to this powerful business model.

Dr. William Chen

General Manager (Hong Kong), Food & Beverage Group

Adjunct Professor, Griffith University

Chapter 1

Introduction to Franchising

> You may be very professional, but that doesn't mean you will have a successful franchise. The franchise itself is a business that requires specific expertise.
>
> —Jules Lederer

How can small- and medium-sized enterprise (SME) entrepreneurs compete effectively with large companies in the market? How can we achieve rapid growth without large capital? The franchise has become one of the most profitable business models in China. The latest data shows that with the support of franchise headquarters, the chances of successful franchisees are generally above 90 per cent, whereas the chances of success in their own, non-franchise businesses are only about 10 per cent. Therefore, franchising has become a rapid expansion of commercial territory and the preferred way to safely start a business.

Maybe you are curious about why it is particularly easy to succeed in franchising. Franchising is a kind of wealth creation method combining entrepreneurship and creativity. The success of franchising requires not only one person to have comprehensive management ability but also the support of entrepreneurship.

To be successful in franchising, the levels of structure, organisation, systems, training, and support are indispensable. In order to understand the success of franchising, you must keep in mind it is a unique business growth strategy and therefore has a unique set of rules.

When you decide to follow the steps outlined in the following sections, you will learn a new business. Beginners are like caterpillars that eventually turn into a colourful butterfly as they go through the book. Jules Lederer, founder of Budget Rent-A-Car System, Inc., learned an important lesson through repeated experiments: "You may be very professional, but it doesn't mean you will have a successful franchise. The franchise itself is a business that requires specific expertise."

In fact, the team behind the franchisers requires an extremely professional team of lawyers, accountants, strategic planners, and experts in sales, operations, and marketing, which is a broad business science. At this point, readers may wonder how these professionals help the business. As an example, one might expect to make a request when launching and selling a new concept, at which point it is important that a lawyer provides a professional opinion. Blindly entering the fog of franchising is like trying to fly over the Bermuda Triangle without radar. But if you follow the right direction, franchising can achieve your wealth aspirations faster than any other growth system.

Are you determined to become a franchiser? Are you ready to take the flight over the Bermuda Triangle? Let's go!

The Origin of Franchising

When it comes to franchising, one must talk about the success of the Singer Sewing Machine Company. In 1865, the Singer Company developed an advanced sewing machine, but it encountered difficulties in sales. The department store was not available to provide technical support. It only relied on the sales representative to go out and tell customers about the sewing machine's various functions. However, the founder had no funds to hire a large number of salespeople, and so commission-based agents were the best sales choice. But it also restricted the development of the company. In this dilemma, Singer decided to recruit franchisees internationally who independently invested to establish sales points. The Shengjia-trademarked sewing machine was authorised by the company for franchisee sales, and Singer was responsible for guiding the franchisees' sales skills. It is not difficult to guess the ending of the story. Due to the adoption of this new business model, consumers quickly accepted Singer Company products, and sales increased greatly. This is the prototype of the franchise.

The Development of Franchising Can Be Divided into the Following Periods

1. Franchising in the Early Twentieth Century

Many people may not know that franchising was first used in the automotive and petroleum industries. Their success opened the door to other retail industries, such as the development of the Benjamin Franklin's General Merchandise Store in 1920 and the emergence of A&W Root Beer in 1925.

2. Franchising in the 1950s

Post-war economic prosperity and rapid development of the interstate highway network caused many industries to spring up. Many entrepreneurs who wanted to take the express train to success had to expand their market share in a short time without using excessive money. The franchise was exactly their antidote. This stimulated the development of franchising in the restaurant, gas station, and other industries. The two fast-food restaurants Hong Kong people love most are increasing at this time. In 1950, Harland David Sanders began his first Kentucky Fried Chicken (KFC) franchise store and established more than six hundred chain stores in ten years. Raymond Albert "Ray" Kroc bought the formula to a small burger stall in San Bernardino, California. The owners of the restaurant were Maurice "Mac" McDonald and Richard "Dick" J. McDonald. Kroc encouraged the McDonald brothers to expand its philosophy in a franchise manner and founded McDonald's in 1959. By the early 1990s, more than 16,000 stores had been established in eighty countries and regions around the world. More than 200 million hamburgers are sold every day, with an annual turnover of 15 billion US dollars.

3. Franchising in the 1960s

In just five years, from 1964 to 1969, guess how many new companies started to use franchising? The numbers are amazing: 100,000. Between 1969 and 1973, another 50,000 companies began to franchise. In 1968, the franchise industry set a sales record of $100 billion, accounting for about 10 percent of US national income.

4. Franchising in the 1970s

In the early 1970s, franchising in Hong Kong began to develop formally from large-scale chain restaurants in the United States. The first franchise store to open in Hong Kong was KFC, introduced in the 1970s, and it still exists. Although Hong Kong people could not accept fried food at the time, KFC returned to Hong Kong again after the 1980s. KFC still accommodates the tastes and preferences of the Hong Kong people.

5. Franchising in the 1980s

In 1981, the franchise whirlwind officially hit Hong Kong. The Dairy Farm Company obtained the Hong Kong franchise of 7-Eleven and began its franchise business, enabling 7-Eleven to expand rapidly in Hong Kong. So 7-Eleven is considered a pioneer in introducing the franchise approach to Hong Kong.

6. Franchising in the 1990s

The ageing of a generation born during the population explosion, the increase in the number of women joining the workforce, the growth of the retirees, and the continuing trend of double-income families required franchising to provide services. Japan City (JHC) started its business in the millennium in North Point in 1991 and has about three hundred branches in Hong Kong and overseas. The current business strategy is "Far, distance; near, attack." That is, Hong Kong will be converted into a self-operated store. It will start with a street shop and then gradually enter the shopping mall. The overseas market will retain the franchise model and establish a sales network in the target market. The Sunshine Laundry Convenience Store Co., Ltd., founded in 1993, has more than sixty stores. It only operated laundry shops in the early days of the business. It was eclipsed in the first two years and only improved in the third year. In 2002, its business development encountered bottlenecks, and so they started to develop a franchise business. How many more can you name in Hong Kong with its countless franchise brands?

What Is a Franchise?

Now that you know the origin and development stories of the franchise, you have a basic concept of this business model. In general, franchising has these characteristics.

1. Franchising is a contractual relationship between a franchiser and a franchisee.

2. Franchisers allow franchisees to use their trade names and/or trademarks and/or service marks, business practices, commercial and technical methods, continuity systems, and other industrial and/or intellectual property rights.

3. Franchisees invest in and own their own businesses.

4. Franchisees pay fees to franchisers.

5. Franchising is a continuous relationship.

Benefits of Franchising

To make franchising a winning business model, you should carefully evaluate the benefits of having a franchise before deciding to purchase one.

Advantages

✓ Having a franchise allows you to be in business for yourself.

✓ The franchise provides a degree of independence for franchisees so they can run their businesses.

✓ Franchisers provide products or services that already enjoy a wide range of brand awareness, giving their franchisees and customers confidence and providing the credibility that takes years to build.

✓ Franchising increases your chances of business success because you are using proven products and methods.

✓ A franchise can provide consumers with a consistent quality in a product or service because it is contractually associated with the established franchiser.

✓ Franchising provides important support before opening a store:

- site selection
- design and construction
- financing (in some cases)
- training
- grand opening project

✓ Franchising provides continuous support:

- training
- country and regional advertising
- operational procedures and assistance
- continuous monitoring and management support
- increased purchasing power through bulk purchases (in some cases)

Hong Kong Franchise Brands Fall into Three Broad Source Categories

1. International franchise brands. Many companies in Hong Kong have become regional licensors of international franchise brands in greater China. They are responsible for finding franchisees in Hong Kong and China and establishing franchise stores such as Yoshinoya and Ajisen Ramen.

2. Hong Kong local brands, such as Storefriendly, Bossini.

3. Mainland franchise brands. Quanjude, Little Sheep Group Limited, Carpenter Ta, and other mainland franchise brands have set up their bases in Hong Kong.

From an industry perspective, it mainly involves the catering, service, and retail industries.

1. Catering industry: Western-style fast food; Chinese fast food; Chinese and Western mixed fast food; Chinese, Western Japanese, and Korean restaurants; coffee shops; bread and pastries; desserts; ice cream. Some examples are Tong Pak Fu and La Kaffa Coffee.

2. Retail: convenience stores, clothing, jewellery, and glasses. Examples include 7-Eleven, Icon Lady, Muse Fashion, and Kura Chika.

3. The service industry: tourism, photo printing, mini warehouse, laundry, beauty, tutoring/education, fitness, leisure interest classes. Examples include Fotomax, Storage Easy Mini Warehouse, Sunshine Laundry Convenience Store, Modern Education, and Dr I-Kids.

Who Should Read This Book?

Successful Entrepreneurs

No mistake, successful entrepreneurs want to make their business stronger, and they can't ignore this rule. A successful entrepreneur must be a dreamer, but a good idea is not enough to launch a successful franchise plan. Similarly, we see that even if we provide mediocre products or services (such as a firm system) through franchising, entrepreneurs' dreams can be rapidly developed, expanded, taught, and replicated into systems, which can greatly increase the chances of entrepreneurs' success.

SMEs at a Crossroads

If you are a small and medium-sized business owner at a crossroads, you may be able to reorganise your distribution channels and regain power through dramatic acquisitions, mergers, and company restructurings, but stop and think about it. How can you have money? The franchise model can share the costs and risks. The only consideration is to take care of the interests of the franchisees. Jollibee, a fast-expanding Philippine fried chicken chain in Hong Kong, in May 2018 plans to acquire Asia-Pacific's district franchise of famous star dim sum shop Tim Ho Wan for $33.5 million (about 260 million Hong Kong dollars). In June 2017, Growth Enterprise Market's shares, Huangpu (8,300), announced that they had jointly acquired two Hong Kong franchisers of Du Hsiao Yuen, a well-known Taiwanese brand. If your business has two or three stores, and you want to know how to expand to by 100 or 1,000, the franchise can provide you with the money you need before others can get there. Pearl milk tea is famous all over the world, and TP Tea is a Taiwanese pearl milk tea brand familiar to Hong Kong people. At present, the number of stores in Taiwan has exceeded 250, and there are also 14 overseas stores. In terms of overseas markets, they are currently stationed in Hong Kong, Shanghai, Singapore, California, and Tokyo and will enter the Vietnamese market in August this year. Then look at companies or stores that follow the traditional way through opening own stores, and you'll find that they haven't achieved half of their growth most of the time because franchising provides a way to quickly enter the market and increase their share.

Business Decision Makers

Franchises seem to be only popular in fast food chains. Is this really true? Amongst the franchise projects in Hong Kong, local projects account for about 56 per cent. By industry, about 43 per cent are engaged in the catering industry, 20 per cent are engaged in the retail industry, and 37 per cent are providing other services such as education centres and laundries. Franchising not only helps small companies, but when the company grows larger, it can be a catalyst to help big companies grow bigger. Many local brands such as the Storefriendly, the Conduct Chinese Medicine Clinic, and Quality Dry-clean have adopted a franchise model to expand the local market with the financial resources and network of franchisees. Some local brands have opened up the mainland market with a franchise model. Chow Tai Fook had 2,358 jewellery outlets in mainland China at the end of September 2017, 39 per cent of which are operated by franchisees.

Franchising allows large companies to expand rapidly, minimising capital resources, and eliminating the need to deploy large numbers of resources. This is a quick ticket to seize market share, enabling companies to penetrate new markets while reducing management costs and costs and decentralising management to the store level. Franchising also provides an innovative way to refinance, allowing management to manage the management of these stores to purchase franchises, which can generate real-time cash flow and ongoing income. Therefore, it is hoped that corporate decision makers, including CEOs, marketing presidents, and professional managers, can better consider expansion through franchising, which provides a good opportunity for companies with a sense of expansion.

Franchisers Seeking Improvement

Yes, this book is highly recommended for franchisers seeking to improve their existing franchise plans. If you already have a franchise, you may not be aware of the magnitude and speed of this industry change. Franchising is not only the most efficient rapid expansion system, but it's also one of the fastest-changing business systems. If you want to run forever at the cutting edge, continuous learning is the only way. In this book, I will share with you the latest information about franchising in order to help you.

Investors, Investment bankers, and Lenders

Investors and lenders cannot ignore the business opportunities and explosive income that franchising brings to you. After all, franchising is a growth-oriented business system, and growth is the whole of investment. Financiers most often manage two main levels: by providing funds to franchisers, and by providing funds to franchisees. The franchise capital needs vary, not for seed capital but for the second phase of expanding capital. Although franchisers may lack collateral or asset value before development, there are still many banks that can provide franchisers with loan support. For example, Royal Bank of Canada supplies franchisers loan support with more than $400 million.

Future Franchisees

Suppose you want to take the test tomorrow. Don't you want to know the test questions before the test? The same is true for those interested in buying franchises. As a franchisee, you should be familiar with at least the basics and a thorough understanding of the franchise agreement itself, including its structure and reasons. In addition, franchisees need to understand their franchise plans, usually marketing, franchise fees, and royalties, group purchases, and cooperative advertising, training, and support.

Women Who Want to Start a Business

There is a saying in Hong Kong that women are most afraid of marrying the wrong man, and men are most afraid of getting into the wrong line. But in today's society, the wrong situation does not happen only to men but also to women. Women are born with strong organisational and coordinating power, and they are good at communicating with people. It is a natural advantage to invest in franchise business. Therefore for sisters who are interested in making a career, how to choose the right franchise brand is no less important than choosing a life partner. The best is not necessarily the best. How can one find the most suitable one from the brand? I believe that after reading this book, you will have enough ability and knowledge to decide.

General Readers

Franchising is one of the most important economic developments of the twentieth century, and it is also a manifestation of a larger social trend. Franchising allows more people to easily own their own business, which makes it easy for these people to climb the corporate ladder and take the company route. At the same time, franchising enables business owners of smaller companies to compete with large companies in the market. Franchising has promoted rapid growth, and even if it is not a large amount of money, as long as it is a well-run enterprise, it has more expansion opportunities than ever before. Franchising is also fascinating because of its changes. It is constantly being applied to new areas in various ways, regardless of size. Anyone interested in this should study franchising, and this book will definitely open the horizon for you, perhaps even providing the opportunity to change your life.

Chapter 2

Have Power of International Brand

"Money, people, time. These three factors will largely determine the success or failure of the expansion plan. They are the three criteria for measuring your expansion plan. Franchising is a rapid expansion without the need for large staff, time and limited capital."

Pre-expansion Considerations

When a company can hardly develop and wants to seek a breakthrough in performance, what will entrepreneurs do? It may be that the product is started, or it may be working hard on the structure, but I believe that a more positive approach must be expansion. For many companies, the problem of expansion is no different from the question of choosing a career for a student. Everyone agrees that this requires a lot of thinking and research. However, most of us are very impulsive, and it is easy to fall into this dilemma.

Readers of this book, you are more cautious in this regard than many businessmen. Before making a decision, you have a willingness to learn and learn a new type of business extension method.

First, I suggest you review all types of business development models (not just franchise) if you don't know much about the different models. This chapter will try to help you with this task. But before considering the expansion method, it is highly recommended that you answer some key questions about your own business.

1. What is your goal? When do you want to open your first store?

2. What is the potential of your expansion concept? Can you copy it quickly and in large quantities?

3. What are the financial and operational capabilities of your business? How much load management can you handle?

If you own this business, you should first consider your personal goals. Do you want to increase the value of your business so that it can be sold within five years? Or do you want to pass it to your child?

Suppose you want your business to grow. When you think about franchising, there is one important question to ask: Are you willing to learn a new business? The need to be a franchiser is different than being an entrepreneur. You and your franchisee have a different relationship with you and your employees. In fact, it is more appropriate to describe the relationship between you and your customers. If you like your current role, you may not like your role as a franchiser.

By asking certain questions, you can help you set your company's goals. For example:

- Is your company's policy conservative or positive? Is it satisfied with slow and steady growth, or is it preparing for a more adventurous future?

- Will your company exist on an existing scale for the foreseeable future? Do you still need to increase market share to survive?

- Is your growth plan controlled by a conservative investor or by a proactive investor?

- Does your manager adapt to new ideas and new business methods?

These issues may cause variables in your expansion plan before any expansion plans are made.

Before continuing, it is better to imagine that if you wake up tomorrow, you will suddenly get the funds you need to expand—such as the amount of money you need to create the largest number of stores the market can afford. In addition, sufficient and experienced management personnel are obtained. Finally, imagine the market conditions remain the same when you complete the expansion plan. How many branches or other types of distribution channels can you build under these optimal and completely unbelievable conditions?

Before you answer, please take a good look at your business. If your company has established a multi-million-dollar resort, how many stores can you actually own under the above conditions? A hundred, five hundred, or ten thousand? Regardless of the answer, now you have a bottom line on the company's potential. If your goal is to maximise this potential, at least you need a comprehensive expansion plan.

Let us go back to reality. Assuming that your company has the potential to build five hundred stores in Hong Kong, and that there are many opportunities in the world, then what capabilities do you have to implement this potential plan? First of all, how much money can you use for expansion? Although some forms of expansion are cheaper than others, do you have enough money to generate five hundred stores? If not, where would you get it?

In addition to funds, what other factors do you think is important? It is a talent. Do you have the right people and enough people to supervise your expansion? If not, where and how do you find these people?

It's perhaps a little more realistic to discuss the most fair thing: time. How much time do you have? Can you catch up with the five hundred stores before the market changes or before the competitors enter the market? Many people think that their business ideas are unique, or at least different.

But in this age of information, the "new" concept will be outdated before they are fully developed.

Money, people, and time—these three factors will largely determine the success or failure of the expansion plan. Therefore they are the three criteria for measuring your expansion plans. To be frank, this book is about franchising because franchising is a way to expand quickly without the need for large staff, time, and limited capital. But before discussing the advantages of franchising in detail, how many types of expansion methods are there? The following will be announced for everyone to see if you have broadened your gaze.

Company-owned Store

What is the most common way of expansion for traditional companies? It is to increase the stores owned by the company. The company provides all funds, fully controls the expansion plan, and retains all profits. Many companies are satisfied with the growth brought about by this approach, but this growth limit is very limited. The cost of adding a new store could be $100,000 or $5 million. The question is: How many stores can the company fund in a year? What opportunities exist? How much debt can you afford? Or, on the contrary, how much business are you willing to give up in order to achieve the expansion plans?

It is clear that the degree of expansion will be limited by the amount of cash that the company has. In addition, there are other shortcomings in establishing a company-owned store. You should also be aware that there is a key factor not mentioned above. If you have not paid attention, you can look at it again, or you can let me tell you: the answer is the talent.

Finding and retaining a good manager is a difficult and time-consuming process.

The further the location spreads, the more serious the situation. Moreover, as noted above, while retaining all the profits of each store, there is also the responsibility for the daily management of each store. Of course, motivating managers through performance-linked incentives is one of the best ways, but the sales volume of a store will stabilise sooner or later, and so the manager realises that he won't get rich but accepts it as part of his salary. At that time, the incentive plan for the manager lost its effectiveness, and the manager's performance deteriorated and even found another way out.

How much profit can a manager bring to the store? How long does it take (and to what extent) to recover the investment cost? In the retail industry, assuming annual sales of $300,000, the store's corporate supervision costs must be paid in full, and the return on investment can take three to four years, or it may end in a loss. In contrast, franchise stores that generate the same revenue can generate $15,000 in royalties each year. In addition, the previous franchise fee will be received, the supervision fee paid will usually be one-third lower than the company-owned store, and the risk of ownership will be borne by the franchisee.

Historically, in the late 1960s and early 1970s, the famous McDonald's also faced management problems. McDonald's CEO Fred Turner decided to significantly increase the number of stores the company has. In 1967, the figure was less than 10 per cent. When the company had a store that reached one-third of all stores, the company began to find serious management problems, and so it decided to reduce the number of stores owned by the company to 25 per cent. The company's policies were maintained. As a multinational corporation, McDonald's has huge assets and effective supervision mechanism, both domestically and internationally. It can be seen that it is not easy to increase the company's own stores. McDonald's learned from experience how excited operators are at the store level and how expensive it is to have control over all stores.

After all, the company needs new money to invest in talents, and so it takes a long time to successfully open a branch.

Partner

Another method of expansion is partnership. Partners can be tempting, especially when they bring the cash they need to their business. When partners have the ability and complement each other, they work well. But based on historical experience, there are very few successful partnerships. When partners find that people have very different ideas about how the business should operate and what the goals should be, the friendship that sustains the partnership will eventually become a disaster. For those who rely on corporate income, nothing is more frustrating than knowing that your partner is doing business badly.

The arrangement of general partners or limited partners avoids some of the dangers of traditional partnerships because the roles of each partner are clearly specified in advance. General partners are usually responsible for managing the business and raising the necessary funds from the limited partners. In return, the limited partner receives most of the income and any tax benefits that may arise. However, current tax laws have minimised these advantages. Typically, partners retain a small portion of the management fee, which is between 10 and 50 per cent of total sales and corporate profits.

It takes cost to set up such a partnership, and so finding a good partner can be very difficult and costly.

Sony Ericsson, a once popular mobile phone brand, is a powerful example of partnership. In August 2001, Sony and Ericsson officially joined Sony Ericsson Mobile Communications to seize the mobile phone market. In addition to funds, they also invested in their own unique technologies and platforms to make their brand calls fascinating. Partnerships do provide the money you need, but they also sacrifice a lot of control. To change the business, you need the consent of the partner. Failure to obtain timely consent may result in the loss of ability to respond to changing market conditions. As we all know, the mobile phone ushered in an epoch-making change in 2007. The system cannot keep up with the pace of response, and coupled with the rise of rising stars, that resulted in serious business losses. This unprecedented partner was eventually acquired by Sony in February 2012. Ericsson's 50 per cent stake ended.

It is hard to say how long it takes to find a partner. The length of time required is hard to say, let alone how long the partnership can last, and both sides must sacrifice some control.

Dealer/Distribution Rights

Of course, the type of expansion discussed in this book is the expansion of the company's distribution network (as opposed to increasing the size or growth of existing facilities through mergers and acquisitions). Traditionally, companies that distribute products have expanded through existing distribution channels, such as independent resellers and distribution channels. But this is obviously not effective; otherwise, franchise will not be born. Many companies find it difficult to motivate and control these distributors or distributors, especially in highly competitive industries. Dealers who offer product choices may consider companies that offer large advertising budgets and subsidies, and profit is always the most important. This is the iron rule of the business world even if your product or service is superior. The advantage is you don't have to say more, and you can guess.

As a result, you will find that your expansion plan can only stay in the gestation stage.

Take a test of yourself. Which of the dealer or franchise is more ancient? The answer is as old as it is. Historically, the control of franchisees is not as loose as an independent dealer, but it provides a business system. In recent years, some manufacturers have been turning dealers into franchisees, providing extensive training, marketing support, and business system incentives in proprietary areas where non-franchisees are not qualified.

This method is not too time-consuming because for distributors, selling more than one brand of products represents a little more business, but it is only necessary for distributors to provide more incentives for you to sell.

For example, Osim, which is famous for selling massage chairs, has more than thirty sales outlets in Hong Kong, including self-operated stores and dealers. However, Osim is also actively recruiting franchisees. The franchisees are more concerned about their own business. After all, they are investing themselves, and they only sell products of a single brand. They can concentrate more research than dealers, and their natural performance is better. The head office is also happy to see this result and naturally recruits franchisees.

License Authorisation

There is an expansion method that is easily confused with the franchise, which is authorisation, but in fact there is a difference between the two.

Franchising is a way of doing business by which an individual or company has the right to offer, sell, or distribute goods or services under the franchiser's marketing plan or system, and to share the franchiser's trademarks, names, labels, and advertisements.

In a traditional licensing arrangement, the licensor only authorises the licensee to use the licensor's name on the product, business, or recipe without substantial management of the licensee's business. For example, Coca-Cola allows manufacturers to place Coca-Cola's name and logo on

T-shirts, but Coca-Cola does not stipulate how manufacturers will make, distribute, or market the T-shirts.

Still don't understand? To put it simply, all franchises contain at least one license, but not every license is a franchise.

A license is a multi-billion-dollar industry that companies can enter at a relatively low cost. The rewards can be amazing. For example, designers such as Bill Blass, Pierre Cardin, and Yves Saint Laurent earned millions of dollars within a year by licensing their names. Reward is certainly attractive, but the shortcomings are obvious. Any company with a licensor's name or trademark may be used to make poor quality products and damage the company's image.

It can be seen from the above examples that this method is successful. The limitation in time is whether the reputation of the brand or the person itself is sufficient. Simply speaking, it is to determine the length of time to establish the fame to determine the time. As far as money is concerned, it depends on how and how long it takes to build a reputation.

If you are looking for a license, you must ask yourself the business question: Can I really allow the licensee to use my name without controlling his entire operating system? Does it seriously affect the quality of goods and services sold under my name? If you decide to let your business expand, then your licensee must do business in the prescribed way. If the licensee pays more than five hundred dollars in six months, and you are willing to let him use your name (even if you don't ask him to do so), you may have already sold a franchise. Of course, you can continue to call it a license.

Sales Representative

Companies, especially manufacturers, can expand their business by creating an employee sales force or hiring an independent contractor as a sales representative. However, many of the ultimate corporate leaders such as Ray Kroc and Jules Lederer do not value sales representatives.

Good sales representatives are hard to find. Providing adequate training, incentives, and compensation and training personnel time is also an important cost, which also makes the company's sales staff very expensive. The greater the sales force, the more dispersed the sales point, and the more serious all these problems. And why? Because the best salespeople are often working alone.

As a value-added reseller for medical and legal professionals in computer hardware and software at International Business Machines Corporation (IBM), Continental Data Systems was sold to twenty-five regional franchises in the first year, which excused the need to hire salespeople, and they have access to markets where companies may not be able to enter. The franchisee's motivation comes from its own investment, like an employee working full-time to promote the Continental Data Systems.

Cooperative

Some independent companies of similar nature will form cooperatives to share the cost of goods and advertising. In Hong Kong, the term *cooperative* is probably stranger to foreigners. There are relatively many foreign countries, but Hong Kong is a cosmopolitan city. There are also cooperatives introduced by foreign countries. It is easy to think of like the Best Western Hotel. The organisation consists entirely of independently owned companies that use the name of Best Western Hotel to provide advertising and in-stock services without controlling them. In addition to the difficulty of forming such a chain, cooperatives have two distinct shortcomings. First of all, although the cooperative may be helpful to join the association's personal stores or existing chain stores, it is not intended to promote the growth of independent owners' branches. Therefore, it is necessary to open a branch for itself through the cooperative method, which is the same as the company owns the store. Second, in cooperation, the central management authority is empowered by individual members, and the power of the organisation is severely restricted. In contrast, franchisees can introduce new concepts and make them part of the entire franchise process.

Sales Consulting Service

Selling expertise and successful experience is also a way for people who want to build a similar business because it can be a source of income. Moreover, it takes a lot of time to expand in this way, but it is advised that it is not good to sell to people in the same district. Otherwise, you are creating competitors for yourself. Although the risk of consultant is small, rewards are very limited.

For example, owners of The Baby's Room, which sells more than $25 million a year, sell their services in this way for a while. Can you guess what the outcome will be? Undoubtedly the result was disastrous. When they saw their "student" using the business system they invented and the performance jumping progressively, they realised that they had indirectly supported many competitors.

As you might expect, all of the above will lead to the question: What is the best way to scale? For many of our readers, the answer will be found in the next chapter.

Chapter 3

Assess the Franchising Suitability for Your Business

> The failure rate of franchising is 5% or less per year, while the failure rate of new businesses is estimated to range from 65% to 90%.
>
> —US Department of Commerce

In the first chapter, we talked about the benefits of franchising and the reason why franchising can become the most popular form of business expansion in the twentieth century. In chapter 3, we objectively reveal its advantages and disadvantages to readers.

Advantages

Capital

As we said, franchising is an expanded approach that allows companies to expand rapidly with minimal capital. So where do successful companies get funding expansion? Some companies choose to sell stocks to get funds, which of course give up a certain amount of autonomy and control.

Some entrepreneurs choose to find bank loans, but banks need corporate collateral. By selling franchises, you don't have to give up control over your business or assets.

Motivated Manager

Every business owner knows that a good manager is just like an ideal partner. If you find it, you have to pay a considerable price for training, and a good incentive system helps excellent managers to develop their greatest abilities. In this book, I hope to teach some secret tactics to those franchisers who have established several branches so that they can sell several stores to the manager of the company in the future, thus creating a good feeling amongst the employees of the entire company, and at the same time creating a satisfactory franchise atmosphere.

A motivated manager benefits the franchiser in three ways.

1. The franchisee represents a consumption pattern of a community or a group, and it also represents a commitment to the community, which determines the degree of consumer participation in the franchise brand.

2. As entrepreneurs develop a franchise business model, motivated managers will hire familiar teams, and the cost of mismatching human resources can be greatly reduced, thereby increasing profitability.

3. A motivated manager is free to operate their franchise store, increasing efficiency and reducing bureaucracy.

Readers can feel it easy to understand when they hear it. There are many examples in Hong Kong. Let me give you an example of the United States. Domino's Pizza has created a satisfactory franchisee in the university town. Domino's hires part-time students at the school and successfully trains them to become managers. These students are well managed, and Domino's allows them to become franchisees. If they don't have $80,000 to $110,000 to open their own Domino's stores, Domino's will help them, but the only requirement is to hold at least 51 per cent of the store's shares. After one year, these young managers have successfully completed the comprehensive training of Domino's and have a franchise.

Purchase Power

As the saying goes, people are more powerful, and in the franchise industry, this is also true. As franchise growth grows, franchisers can help franchisees reduce the cost of equipment and incoming goods in the form of at least 10–20 per cent group discounts on the grounds of large volume, which is an unprecedented, collective buying advantage. As a franchiser, you may only want to invest a portion of your money in technology development. Another collective buying advantage of franchising is to help franchisees better use funds to reduce spending on advertising and public relations. Imagine that when a franchiser advertises on TV, all stores with the same name will also be responsive, which is a cumulative effect that helps to increase the direct competition of franchise store for other small businesses.

History never lies. There are three fast food giants in the United States: McDonald's, Burger King, and Wendy's. They are also making low-priced and traditional hamburgers. You think ordinary fast food restaurants have the ability to price that low? Is it better than them? What do you think is the reason for franchisers to achieve long-term monopoly in the market? It is the advantage of collective purchase! Another reason is the franchise TV commercial. In 1986, McDonald's spent about $525 million on advertising, and these funds are also from the franchisee's joining fees. The result of the annual sales of a McDonald's store averaged $1.3 million, and advertising revenue 4 per cent, or about $52,000 a year. For a fast food restaurant, this is a considerable income, and as a franchise store with 6,000 or more stores, the annual sales of each store increased by $52,000. Counting how much performance you have in total, you can see how effectively advertising can make McDonald's return to the book and even make money, and this has become a cost-effective TV commercial for McDonald's. So do you find that joining a franchise system can make your store bigger and faster?

Income

Strictly speaking, most franchisers can earn revenue from six sources in addition to sharing profits with franchisees.

1. Initial franchise fee
2. Royalties
3. Advertising fee
4. Selling products to franchisees
5. Sell additional services to franchisees
6. Property lease

The advertising fee has been explained in the previous point, and the initial franchise fee is a one-time admission fee for the franchise plan, which covers the cost of franchise marketing and training, site-assisted assistance, sales commission, and store assistance.

Revenue is earned by franchisers from royalties, typically ranging from 4 to 20 per cent of total sales. It is a franchise fee that franchisers must continue to support their franchisees so that the appropriate franchise fees are important, are not too high or too low, and are negotiated by both parties.

Franchisers can sell products to franchisees, typically selling products that are closely related to the business itself, and prices and quality are not readily available elsewhere. Better franchisers will provide franchisees with accounting, human resource management, real estate negotiations, and production equipment, which will help monitor the operation of franchisees. This tailor-made service is a good choice for franchisees.

Founded in 1972, the French beauty brand Guinot was originally producing its own beauty products and providing beauty treatments. With the expansion of the company's scale, more than 10,000 beauty centres and spas around the world use their branded treatments. In 2010, Guinot became a franchiser and sold 800–1,000 franchises worldwide, except for regular franchisees. In addition to beauty training, Guinot sell their own products and open source for themselves.

In the long run, the success of the franchise depends on the success of the franchisee. If the franchisee is unsuccessful, the system will collapse. On the contrary, if they succeed, the franchise sales can be very fast. Although the franchisers' income is not directly related to the franchisees' profitability, don't forget that the entire franchise plan itself ultimately depends on the franchisees' profitability.

Location

Is the impact of location huge on profit earning? The answer is yes, unless you have the confidence to rely on yourself to drive the flow of people throughout the region. If the brand you run is highly focused on the location, the franchise model can help you convince the mall owners and developers. See the business opportunities, thus giving you a more favourable entry price.

Flexibility

Regardless of the company's situation, structure, and objectives, with limited financial resources, franchisers can get start-up funds to build stores, hire employees, and manage day-to-day operations. The franchise can also be flexible in another direction. If you are short of funds but have good management skills, you can let your franchisees go all out and provide them with your management services. Perhaps you are curious as to how it works. In fact, this is a great way to attract multi-store investors, because you can attract some people who have the money, can support your concept, and have the potential to invest in you. This management model is very common in the hospitality industry to help small companies grow, whereas the franchise system can operate efficiently and achieve better returns in companies with more resources and expectations.

Exit Strategy

Another advantage of franchising is to increase the overall market value of the business. What is its added value? It is the store network, coverage, occupancy, customer base, and more. If your brand is intentionally acquired after five to ten years, you should take a look at the franchise, which makes this business a valuable asset.

Of course, everything has both positive and negative sides. This book will also objectively list the shortcomings of franchising so that readers should not make this choice when considering expansion.

Disadvantages

Out of Control

The biggest single drawback of franchising is the loss of control. For franchisers, there are two risks to bear.

First, franchisees will not be able to operate as they do. The complexity of operating a business is not small, and it is difficult to fully teach franchisees within an acceptable time. Many of the franchisers provide a complete training system to solve this problem. For example, 7-Eleven convenience stores in Hong Kong provide sixty to ninety days of training to new franchisees, and training will be provided from time to time during the operation period. However, franchisers rarely train franchisees for more than thirty days; two weeks is more common, and time is never enough.

The second risk is that franchisers will have difficulty accepting the loss of control. Some business owners, who want to reduce their participation in daily operations, eventually find it very difficult. As a boss, you can tell the manager to change the price, change the layout, and change the inventory, and if you don't like it, you can even change the tie he wore that day. But as a franchiser, you have to deal with advice, motivation, and persuasion, not orders. In fact, being a franchiser for a business can be fun, but it needs to be different from the skills to start an existing business—not risk management and motivation, but to master diplomatic art, become a good listener, and learn to speak publicly. Another aspect of losing control of each store is the issue of price and profit and total sales. Does the franchisee set the retail price too high, pushing customers to competitors? Or is the price too low so that the profits of the franchiser and the franchisee's gross profit are both ambiguous? The franchiser's goal is to maximise profits, but the franchisee's goal, based on the percentage of royalties, is the store's largest sales. Therefore the franchisee may adjust the price, equipment, or labour to increase the total sales without increasing the profit. That is, when the price is raised, the equipment maintenance cost and the labour force (or salary) are also raised to achieve the total sales. The purpose is raising the sales but keeping the same profit.

Conflict and Litigation

Potential conflicts and litigation are indeed another disadvantage of franchising, and most successful franchisers have encountered this problem. Everyone likes to win, but it is impossible to run 100 per cent of any business in this form. According to statistics, there are 5 per cent failures in the business operated by franchise. When franchisees fail to make a profit, you may face allegations of fraud, misrepresentation, inadequate training, and more. The legal costs of protecting yourself from such allegations are enormous.

On the other hand, if you borrow money to expand your business but then fail, your lender may sue you or ask you to pledge with promised collateral. If you have sold the company's equity to investors and lose control of the company, losing your job as a CEO, you may be prosecuted for fraudulent statements. The key to avoiding conflicts and litigation is to choose the right franchisees, give them adequate training and support, properly manage the franchise plan, maintain a good franchisee relationship, and look for industry or economic changes that may affect the business.

Find Qualified Franchisees

What is a qualified franchisee? Everyone has his or her own answer, but what is certain is that a successful franchisee is the backbone of any franchise plan. Attracting and retaining franchisees with the best potential for success is the first step. The franchisee must be financially able to bear the start-up costs of the franchise store, and the high start-up costs will scare away some qualified franchisees. Another thing to consider is that there are thousands of franchise opportunities today, and franchisers must compete with the savviest franchisers for qualified franchisees.

Profitability of Each Store

The percentage of total store profits in all business of the company as a percentage of total sales is the gross profit of the franchiser. What is the percentage? In successful stores, the percentage is much lower than the total profit of the store. Of course, this must weigh the many advantages of franchising, including the franchiser's capital risk, rapid expansion potential, and collective purchasing power. However, due to the different capabilities of each franchisee, the geographical location and the flow of people are different, and there is also the opportunity to have the above-mentioned loss of control, so the franchiser's income is passive.

Changes in the Market

The commercial market is changing rapidly. If the franchiser is not sensitive enough to the market or the industry, the development is backwards or even closed. Take a hamburger fast food restaurant that is familiar to Hong Kong people as an example. The name will not be revealed first, so that readers can guess.

This hamburger fast food restaurant has been in Hong Kong for more than thirty years. Its franchise rights are special. It is regional. The highest peak has about twenty franchise stores. However, it constantly faces new and old rivals, and old rivals continue to introduce new ones. Freshness, new tastes, and new offers have been pushed in and out. Although the french fries are full of praise, the updated menus have not been relegated under the siege, and the food incident has shrunk from about twenty stores to five stores. After knowing it, the chain later renewed its menu and offers, but it eventually lost his soul and closed. Smart readers should have guessed that this fast food restaurant is Burger King.

It can be seen that if the market is not able to maintain the sense of touch, no matter how long the history is, the strength behind it will be strong, and eventually it will be swallowed up by the market.

Unmanageable Growth

For some people, it is too easy to find a franchisee. Even with all the laws protecting future franchisees, once the franchiser creates the number of franchisees that exceeds his management ceiling, the loss will be sudden and dramatic appear.

D'Lites of America, Inc., is an example of growing too fast. D'Lites's store offers low-fat, low-calorie hamburgers, sandwiches, and salads, and Americans' health and weight loss is a successful idea.

In the past four years, D'Lites has opened 86 restaurants, 63 of which were sold to franchisees, but in 1985 it recorded an astonishing deficit, some of which lost as much as $1 million. There are several main reasons for the failure: large chain stores have added healthier menus and salad bars, new franchisees lack sufficient restaurant experience, and franchisers provide insufficient support for training. For franchisees and D'Lites, the seemingly promising governance model failed to materialise. In addition, in order to protect and motivate franchisees, D'Lites has exhausted funds, so the plans that could be used to advertise to consumers are also ruined.

Conclusion

Despite occasional failure examples—and it is certain that some are completely failed—the franchise enjoys an extraordinary record of success. As the US Department of Commerce estimates, the failure rate of franchising is a negligible 5 per cent or less per year, while the failure rate of new businesses is estimated to range from 65 to 90 per cent. This incredible data does not stop critics from discovering other less obvious "disadvantages". Some people will say that because franchising relies on unity and consistency, it promotes mediocrity and stifle personality. However, there is no reason to believe that because the company or product is consistent and reliable, it must be mediocre. In fact, if so, its chances of success will be reduced because consumers will find the best value for them. The franchise system does not stifle creativity. Instead, it encourages entrepreneurs to realise their own ideas and allows others who are less willing to accept such ideas to listen to their success stories.

Franchising is growing at an alarming rate because they give individuals the opportunity to own a business, have security, and have a well-documented company backing. Not every successful business should use a franchise, but given the appropriate circumstances and concepts, it can provide an extraordinary wealth production system for franchised businesses.

Chapter 4

Package Your Concept Uniquely for Franchising

> "Before starting to charter your existing business, consider those company with weak concepts and products but successful franchise. What are their secrets? The answer is their operating system."

Create a Franchise Business

Whether you have a business or just an idea of owning a business, it's important to understand the quality of the franchise's success before deciding to use the franchise as an expansion system. Three broad areas are critical when assessing the franchise capabilities of any business.

1. The concept and structure of the business

2. The vendibility of the business

3. Business capabilities and commitment

Business Concept and Structure

What is the most overrated part of franchising? It is a great new concept. Sound crazy? Think about it: some of the most successful franchise companies have many similarities, and their concepts are not unique. Next question: What is the second overestimation of franchising? It is the quality of a product. For example, the giant hamburger franchise McDonald's, in the consumer survey, has been ranked behind Burger King and Wendy in the vote for the best quality hamburgers in the United States. However, Wendy only accounts for 12 per cent of the three companies, which together account for 72 per cent of the market. The second-placed Burger King accounted for 19 per cent, whereas McDonald's occupied 41 per cent. So before you pledge your house, quit your job, get back all your savings, and start franchising your existing business, consider those franchise companies whose concepts and products are not great but successful. What are their secrets? The answer is their operating system. Amongst the three, McDonald's not only has the largest market share, but it also has the best operating system.

McDonald's always outperforms others because it has better location, layout, consistency, product quality, service speed, advertising, and focus on the children's market. McDonald's has improved store efficiency, reduced costs, and increased self-service vending machines and the ability to place orders with phone apps, turning orders and charges into electronic. The whole concept is easier to succeed.

Prototype

You must have a profitable business prototype before you start a franchise. This may be your main business model for franchising. How long should you operate before creating a franchise? Of course, the longer you build, the higher your credibility. But like concepts and products, history is not a key factor. If you don't have a business and are still at the conceptual stage, you can follow the advice given in this book to build your own company. But no matter which stage you are in, you will be ready to sell the franchise until you find a prototype and generate positive cash flow.

Financial Control

Good financial control is critical to any operating system. If the company are running a messy account and losing money for years, who will join? It is better to use some hardware and software to monitor accounting and performance data in real time. It can even be connected to cameras located in key areas of each store, allowing franchisers to observe remote location operations. Through these systems, you can get the latest registration readings, number of employees on duty, product portfolio, customer accounts, payroll, hours of work, and other relevant information that are critical to business operations and management.

Large companies have different problems. Although financial controls are in place, financial and business functions performed at the enterprise level may need to be transferred to the store level for franchise purposes. Other things will be about the payroll, accounts payable, accounts receivable, purchases, depreciation, general and administrative expenses of individual business units, and differences in the cost of goods.

Regardless of whether the company is large or small, financial and operational reporting systems will be important if the store is located in a remote location—not only for franchise plans but also for existing businesses.

Profitability

When talking about financial matters, I said that the prototype should have positive cash flow. In other words, it is profitable, but what about the profit? It is 15 per cent of the return on investment capital of franchisees. Not 15 per cent of sales, but 15 per cent of return on investment. For example, if a franchisee needs $200,000 to open a store, $30,000 is 15 per cent of that $200,000 investment.

By the way, when it comes to profitability, it refers to the franchisee, not the franchisor. For various reasons, franchisors itself may suffer losses, which are not related to the operation cost. For example, there may be too many employees inside the franchisors, or costs of research and development of new products, even higher wages to hire a manager with higher positions, and a rental cost that is higher than the franchisees. These adjustments need to be taken into account to determine whether there is a credible franchise model.

Marketability of Business

Earlier, I said that how long it takes to open a business is not an important factor in franchising. It is not a must for a company to operate for many years, with a large number of stores and a good reputation, before having an ideal franchise prototype. However, most of the companies that started selling franchises have only one store. It is actually more attractive to potential franchisees because it suggests that the business may be an emerging industry or may be a niche market that caters to the future. Some franchise giants, especially fast food restaurants, find it increasingly difficult to find new locations. The same is true for Starbucks, which owns all of the company's stores. However, Starbucks' success has benefited many individual coffee shop owners who have an ambition to franchise their markets as well.

If concepts and products are not critical, it is important to be able to demonstrate the difference between your business and your competitors when considering franchising. You may have a unique store design, a special marketing plan, a special way of distributing products or services, or a price that is more attractive than your competitors. Sometimes only one differentiation can make you successful. However, mind your competitors, who adjust all the disadvantages, or your advantage will disappear.

If you are still in the concept stage and have not yet established a prototype, make sure your product or service has a market. Introducing a new concept requires a lot of money. Ask yourself before you introduce it: Do you really need this product or service? Can this product or service be explained to people correctly? Is this a good idea? Larger companies have enough resources to have test marketing and focus groups. Take KFC as an example. In China, franchisees provide white porridge fritters for breakfast selection, and they have become regular meals after many studies and trials. In Hong Kong, KFC often has different experimental products. For example, KFC tried to provide shake powder with chicken granules earlier, but the response was not as good as McDonald's, so later you simply don't see it on the official menu.

If you plan to launch your franchise program domestically or internationally, you should first do your homework in the new market and research competitors of the same type of products and services. In the process, you can also understand the opportunities that exist in the market, but the most important thing is not to use franchisees as a trial for testing the feasibility of your concept.

Facilities and Personnel

One of the keys to a successful franchise is your ability to assist franchisees in finding their locations. Sometimes franchisors don't sell franchises unless you have already helped the franchisees find locations, such as in shopping centres. If you have a fast food concept and need a food court, you may find the space in the existing mall very difficult to find. Usually, shopping centre owners provide available locations to other experienced operators because their surplus is larger than the basic rent, and they can pay a certain percentage of the total performance to the mall. Affordability can also be a factor that requires exploration of land costs, liquor licences, construction costs, supplier availability, building codes, personal service permits, legal requirements, political factors, and other issues before entering the market. You also need to be reasonably convinced that the franchisee will find the people you need to run your business. What kind of expertises are you looking for? How many labourers do you need to employ? What is the minimum wage and standard working hours? What is the minimum working age? What is the work culture? To think care about all these factors, you can predict whether your business may not be suitable for certain markets in the worst scenario.

Cultivability

In order to obtain the franchise right, it is important to be able to provide effective and efficient training to your franchisees as early as possible. You must be able to teach franchisees how to serve customers within four to eight weeks, and some franchises require longer training time. For example, at 7-Eleven mentioned in the previous article, the training time is sixty to ninety days, and there are irregular trainings during the operation period, from management shops to sales systems, incoming goods, shelves, and more. It is rare to see 7-Eleven closed, and eventually it develops to "There is always one nearby every customer". In franchising, its success is directly related to the quality, intensity, and duration of training.

Credibility

Creating a successful franchise requires credibility, and the credibility itself comes from the franchisors' story. Any favourable publicity, letters, or even customer reviews will enhance the brand's credibility. News stories about the franchisors' personal achievements—whether it's a business event or a contribution to the community, or video clips from TV broadcasts, or articles from trade publications and national magazines and newspapers—are worth cherishing. If the company's initial brand story is not enough, you may hire public relations companies to design for you. They can attach titles to the company and send it to the relevant news media, which can become an advertisement spread on the Internet or television.

In addition, you also need to regularly read newspapers and magazines related to your industry, as well as update industry quotations and trends. For example, the news reports a chain cake coupon for a chain of cakes is being speculative, and because you are a company that operates related businesses, you can cut this news down and use it for future use as long as the media recognises it.

Cost

The more expensive the franchise business is, the less people are willing to join. In fact, it may not be true because it depends on the ratio of the investment to the total cost of the business. For example, the franchise fee for two different franchise companies is $500,000, but the total cost of A's business is 1 million, whereas B's is $700,000. If the franchise fee is the same, the scale of the business is very different. Which is more worth investing in? The answer is coming. Before starting to sell the first franchise, you should list the sources of financing for franchisees such as from vehicles to equipment, inventors, computers, working capital, large or expensive products, and even credit cards loans. These are important for new franchisees, all of which make franchising more popular and successful.

Ability and Commitment

This book will help you understand the elements of franchising, but more important, whether you have the ability and commitment to dedicate yourself to it. You need to shift your management style from all the "central and radiation" patterns that are directly reported to you to a more structured paradigm, so you should sell and train the top ten direct stores yourself. The father of the modern circus, Phineas Taylor Barnum, once said, "Everyone has been deceived every minute!" The franchise is not to find the deceiver and then charge, provide one or two weeks of training, and finally to wait for the franchisee's gross profit. This is a ridiculous mistake. The correct attitude is about understanding the business scope into which you will enter.

The sale of franchise is the same as the birth of a child. Your responsibility will not end with the birth, but the responsibility begins with the birth. Nurturing, supporting, mentoring, and engaging with the children are your lifelong responsibilities, and the same applies to franchising. The best companies are those that fully understand the need for recruitment, training, and support. Companies such as McDonald's, KFC, and 7-Eleven have successful statistics to verify this practice. Well-prepared franchising applies to everyone: franchisees, suppliers, consumers, and finally franchisors.

Franchise Test

Now you should have an understanding of where your business is between "completely inalienable" and "able to franchise", but with the following short quizzes, you can understand your situation more accurately. Answer the questions below, add your score, and read the results below.

1. Do you have a prototype?

No (1 point)

Yes (10 points)

_____

2. How many stores are you in operation?

1 point per shop, up to 10 points

_____

3. How long has your store been opened?

Not yet in operation (0 point)

Less than half a year (2 points)

A year (4 points)

Two years (6 points)

Three years (8 points)

More than four years (10 points)

_____

4. To what extent is your business different from other competitors?

Not at all (0 points)

A little bit (3 points)

Very (7 points)

Unique (10 points)

_____

5. How much does your store cost, excluding the franchise fee?

$400,000 or more (2 points)

$200,000 to $399,000 (4 points)

$100,000 to $199,000 (6 points)

$50,000 to $99,000 (8 points)

Less than $50,000 (10 points)

_____

6. Your business market is:

Local (0 point)

In the area (3 points)

Nationwide (8 points)

International (10 points)

_____

7. The price of your product or service compared to your competitors:

High (1 point)

Moderate (5 points)

Low (10 points)

_____

8. How systematic is your business?

Not systematic (0 point)

Some policies and/or manuals (2 points)

Very systematic and documented (6 points)

Highly systematic and computerised (10 points)

_____

9. How long does it take to teach others to run your business?

For special certification (1 point)

2 to 6 months (2 points)

1 to 2 months (4 points)

1 to 3 weeks (7 points)

1 week or less (10 points)

_____

10. How does your sales compare to the sales of similar companies?

Much lower (0 point)

Slightly lower (1 point)

About the same (3 points)

Slightly higher (7 points)

Higher (10 points)

Rating

0–39 points

Take a step back and think about it. Your business needs to make significant progress and may need the help of industry experts. If your business has strong rivals in the market, look for ways to improve and grab points in other areas.

40–59 points

Need to fine-tune. You have a promising start; now it's time to start working and make your franchise successful, such as systemising your business, promoting sales, and adding different elements to make your business unique.

60–79 points

Above the standard. You have all the franchise elements of success, and at this point your goal is more like a key factor.

80–100 points

Look at McDonald's! As a concept that cannot be missed, a full franchise can be obtained. Act now!

Chapter 5

Build a Franchise Revenue Plan

> "Running a business can be infinitely separated, that is, to copy and open a branch. A successful company is the first step toward franchising, let others copy your business according to your concept."

Wrap Your Franchise Concept

Once upon a time, did you ever imagine that you know how to split yourself into several identities so that you can do things that you don't like, such as going to school or going to work, while you can enjoy eating and sleeping all day long? Of course, the reality is that people can't be separated, but you can divide your company into different stores. A successful business is not the same as having a franchise. Although a successful business is the first step towards franchising (which is to let others copy your business according to your concept), you need to clearly define your method and business systems.

There are five key areas that must be considered in order to package your concept as a franchise.

1. Define your corporate culture

2. Identify and prepare your business ecosystem

3. Create your unique customer positioning

4. Key support services that must be provided to the franchisee in your system

5. Construct a financial plan

#1: Define Your Corporate Culture

Having a corporate culture is a new definition of the entire franchise ecosystem.

- Who are you?

- Why do you exist?

- How do you want to treat your business ecosystem?

- Who is your consumer?

- Who works for you and your franchisee?

- Who supplies your franchise system?
- Who provide resources for your franchise system?

The clearer the answers to the above questions, the more overwhelming you are in establishing a global standard franchise organisation.

Culture = Dominant attitudes and behaviours characterised by the operation of groups or organisations.

Thinking to Realise Your Corporate Culture

Your goal

- vision
- mission statement
- corporate culture
- business concept
- business principle
- franchise thinking

Exercise: Corporate Culture

Which words best describe your company (no more than ten)?

What is your business philosophy?

What kind of relationship do you want to build with your franchisee?

How do you want to treat customers?

How do you want to treat employees (including team members and your franchisees)?

How do you want to treat suppliers?

#2: Identify and Prepare Your Business Ecosystem

From the very beginning, the company was a vibrant organisation with its own life. Therefore, it is affected by inputs and pressures inside and outside the ecosystem. The ecosystem includes:

1. Customers
2. Employees
3. Supplier
4. People who provide resources (water, electricity, etc.)

This ecosystem is affected by many factors, including:

- competition
- changing trends
- political environment
- national, regional, or global economic environment

Before starting a franchise, you need to evaluate this ecosystem to ensure that all members of the ecosystem have the ability and understanding of your business philosophy.

Business Ecosystem

- client
- employee
- supplier
- lender

Exercise: Your business ecosystem.

List your ecosystem members and place a checkmark next to each member who can grow with you.

- client
- employee
- business ecosystem
- supplier
- person who provides resources

What changes do you need to make to your business ecosystem in preparation for the franchise?

#3: Create Unique Customer Positioning

How to keep customer loyalty is always a profound knowledge. Think about why you fall in love with a brand of cosmetics or perfume, or even food stores. What are their attractions? In order to gain market share, you must find a unique way to attract your customers so that they consume happily.

When it comes to franchising, you must consider another aspect: simplicity. In order for your industry or business for franchisees to replicate effectively, you must simplify your approach.

Suppose your product or service meets the basic quality requirements and can be executed as the customer expects. The first step in determining your unique customer positioning is the customer.

- Who are your customers? Why are they looking for your product?
- How are they going to use your product?
- Where do they want to buy?
- Does your packaging conform to the way customers use the product?
- What are the guarantees for product risk?

Unique Customer Offer

Sales

- What are you selling?
- How did you sell it?

- Who do you sell products to?

Production

- What are you making?
- How did you produce it?
- Where are you producing?
- Who is producing?

Competition

- Who are they?
- What are their methods?
- How do they implement their methods?
- Do they meet market needs?

Exercise: Unique Customer Positioning

The Uniqueness Of Our Sales

What changes will you adapt to your business concept to make it more attractive to franchising?

#4: Critical Support Services

One of the rules of success is that success depends not on oneself but on others. Before franchising, you need to have a way of thinking that the growth and success of a company depends to a large extent on the efforts of the franchisee.

These two areas of support must be considered:

a) support services shared by the franchise

b) companies that need or support your services because of your uniqueness

Both areas have a common goal: What do you have to do in order for your franchisee to succeed?

Common support for franchising

- initial training for franchisees (and their employees)

- initial support related to access to space, financing, initial equipment, initial supply, etc.

- initial support for opening franchise stores and marketing

- ongoing training

- continuous support

- continuous marketing

- continuous research and innovation to maintain brand leadership

Exercise: Key Support to Your Business

Are there any special needs and special types of training and support to make your franchise successful?

Are you ready to take responsibility for supporting your franchisee?

#5: Constructing a Financial Plan

If you are not sensitive to numbers, it is advised to read the following rules several times, because financial health has a critical impact on the success or failure of the business.

The franchisee must ensure that there are sufficient funds and resources before embarking on the franchise. The franchisee must also ensure that they have a clear understanding of the amount the franchisee initially needs to invest and the additional amount needed to maintain and make the new franchise profitable.

This financial plan must answer some of these specific questions.

a) What is the total investment for opening a store?

b) What should be the initial franchise fee?

c) What other initial costs are there? Training? Marketing? Technology?

d) What are the appropriate royalties?

e) Should training, marketing, and technology be charged after the opening of the business?

f) What is the operating break-even point of the business?

g) How long does it take for franchisees to reach this break-even point?

h) What is the best sales level that franchisees can achieve? When is it reached?

i) How much can a franchisee earn in the first year?

Single Store Financial Budget

Start building a financial budget that includes financial information. The first step in the preparation of the financial statements is to use the "store average" financial statements.

- The financial statements are once a month, from the first month to the twelfth month after the operating break-even point.

- Insert the amount of royalties you think is correct (it will be adjusted later).

- Insert all costs of the franchisee without the company infrastructure you may have.

- The fee on marketing, staffing, and technology must be clearly reflected in the financial statements.

- Follow a simple financial statement model.

    1. Sales/monthly income after 1–12 months
    2. Cost of goods balance
    3. gross profit
    4. Labour cost
    5. Occupation cost
    6. Royalty

7. Marketing
8. Technology
9. Interest before interest, tax and tax-related transactions, and interest on trading profits

The second step in completing this financial statement is to determine what working capital the franchisee needs to achieve operational balance. This must include:

- funds required for franchisees to sign a franchise agreement to start business (legal and professional fees, recruitment of key staff costs, training fees, etc.)

- support for the funds needed for the business until the balance of payments

- franchisees need to plan personal household expenses; these figures do not have to be reflected in working capital.

The third step is to determine the initial and operating expenses charged to the franchisee. There are several fees, as follows:

- initial franchise fee

- training costs: franchisees and their employees at the beginning of training

- training costs: training franchisees and their employees in operation

- marketing expenses: selling new stores

- marketing expenses: creating related activities

- technical costs: the technology required to procure and set up franchise operations

- technical fees: technology required to support the operation of the franchise site

The biggest anxiety of franchisees is the setup fee. How much is the initial and ongoing fee for the franchisor to collect franchise fees, royalties, et cetera?

In the absence of any logical method, the franchisor has two choices: to copy other franchisors in the market, or to make arbitrary decisions.

Of course, there is no right or wrong decision on the fees you charge as long as the franchisee is willing to pay. However, these important decisions are best made within a certain framework.

Step four is to determine the initial total investment.

project description: low-end or high-end?

initial franchise fee

training

technology

start marketing

website design

website building

equipment

appliances and fixtures

professional supplies

resale supplies

working capital

total investment

Go or Not Go

Decision Model

The first stage: the applicability of franchising (1 is the lowest, 5 is the highest)

Understand the relationship between franchisors and franchisees (1–5 points)

Have confidence in the success of the replication of the company's store (1–5 points)

There are clear reasons to operate a franchise (1–5 points)

Clear vision of franchising (1–5 points)

The correct attitude of franchising (1–5 points)

Suitability assessment score (1–5 points)

Franchise commitment (1–5 points)

Total in first stage

Above 17 points, it is recommended to enter the second stage. Below 17 points, it is recommended to re-evaluate in the following stages.

The second stage: package your franchise concept (1 is the lowest, 7 is the highest)

Clear organisational culture (1–7 points)

Identify and prepare your business ecosystem (1–7 points)

Clearly defined unique customer positioning (1–7 points)

Clear and ready to support franchisees (1–7 points)

Financial solutions are meaningful to franchisees (1–7 points)

The second stage in total

Chapter 6

Learn the Seven Key Elements to a Replicable Franchise System

> "The franchise design ensures a consistent product, service, and experience for the customer, providing a similar experience for the customer and bringing similar results to the franchisee."

The following is a practical roadmap essential to franchise your business.

1. Business and financial models
2. Trademarks and legal documents
3. Operation manual
4. Franchisee training program
5. Franchise recruitment system
6. Franchise support plan
7. Infrastructure, technology, and supply chain

Construct Seven Elements of a Replicable System

Element 1: Business and Financial Models

As a business owner, expanding business is inevitable, and franchising is a fast and low-investment business expansion method, but what is the most important thing for franchisors and franchisees? It is sustainability. Therefore, it is necessary to create a clear business plan for the franchise and the financial model of the franchise performance (as we did in the previous section). At the same time, detailed business plans and financial models need to be created for the development of franchise companies.

Before a franchisee makes a strategic decision to expand through a franchise, it must first develop a clear strategy that will help develop the business.

- how to recruit new franchisees

- how to train franchisees

- how to support franchisees

- how to innovate

- ensure that appropriate resources (funds, personnel, etc.) are provided in a timely manner to maintain the expansion of the franchise company

- ensure that appropriate resources (funds, personnel, etc.) are provided in a timely manner to maintain the development of the franchise company

The financial model created for the success of the franchisee and the financial model of the franchise store cannot be exactly the opposite.

As for the franchisees who choose to invest in the business, what should be paid attention to? To maintain your enthusiasm, you must have certain expectations for the business, including personal goals, lifestyle goals, and financial goals. At the same time, franchisees rely on franchisors to teach them business and provide ongoing support. There are no industry or business experiences before, and of course there is no unique way you create them.

Although the experience of the company's stores can provide data, it can only be used for reference. Because the company's stores do not operate like independent franchise stores, franchisors and franchisees can gain different experience and resources.

It is important to have a clear plan for the benefit of the franchisee, including:

- how much investment is required to open a store, and how long it takes for the franchisee to pay the license fee

- how to hire people to manage the business, including the competitive compensation needed to find the right people

- if you need a location to run your business, the actual rental rate overhead

- the amount of time each store is open

- length of time the franchisee can get compensation from the company

- actual profit per franchise store per year.

Once the franchisor and franchisee plan has been initially completed, a realistic check is required.

- The franchisor determines the reasonableness of the initial franchise fee and all fees paid by the franchisee. The biggest financial question is if franchisees make the necessary investments and follow the plans listed by the franchisor, will they get the return on investment that is expected previously?

- The franchisor can determine whether the business model is sustainable in the business plan, based on the ongoing fees charged from the franchisee, through which the sustainability of the franchisor and franchisee can be determined.

Note: In order to make the franchisee successful, it is best for the franchisor to give full support to the following plan.

Required Resources

- franchisee's profit plan
- franchisee's monthly financial plan
- franchisee's profit plan
- franchisee's 3- to 5-year financial plan

Element 2: Trademarks and Legal Documents

Trademarks

A good trademark definitely remembers your brand, so your trademark is a valuable asset, especially for franchising, and you must ensure that the trademark is registered and protected.

Trademarks include:

- name (product name) and logo
- service tag
- website
- social media website

It is necessary to decide in the planning as early as possible how the franchisee will promote its business on the network. Who will own the domain name? Who controls the content? Where is the franchise website registered?

At the same time, decisions need to be made on social media sites. Websites such as Facebook and Twitter are part of people's lives, and franchisees need guidance on how to cross their personal and business lives with social media sites.

Legal Documents

The most important legal document is the franchise agreement. Prepare this document to guide you through the creation of a franchise business, including the following business locations:

- agreement period
- initial and operating expenses
- sales reports and miscellaneous payments
- the number of controls that you wish to exercise

- business philosophy and brand promise by which franchisees must abide

- responsibility assigned to franchisees

- expectations for franchisees

- your role and commitment

- training responsibilities of both parties

- how to use the trademark

- how to use the supply chain

- requirements for using proprietary technology or products

- whether the franchisee wants to try new product or service approval policies and procedures

- extended policy

- renewing the franchise agreement

- what events lead to default, and what are the remedies?

- reasons for termination of authorisation

- procedures to terminate authorisation

- confidentiality agreements to maintain document consistency, rather than creating a unique agreement each time a new franchisee is signed

Required Resources

- registration of all trademarks

- registration of all websites

- registration of all social media sites

- franchise agreement and related disclosure documents

Element 3: Operation Manual

Have you ever visited some restaurants with ancestral recipes, secret sauces, and unique methods? These secrets are not the tools they rely on to survive, and as a franchisor, the operation manual is your "unique secret". It reveals to the franchisee how to run your business, and it should include the four Ps related to your business in detail.

- process

- procedure

- policy

- plan

Because each business is dynamic and constantly changing, it must be reviewed quarterly to make the necessary updates and revisions in a timely manner.

Without an operating manual, your business will face the following dilemmas.

- It cannot transfer knowledge about how to conduct business to franchisees.

- Franchisees can act according to their own wishes so that the customer experience is not consistent.

- There is no consistency in branch operations in different locations.

- The franchisee has no influence.

The operation manual needs to be provided in writing during the initial training and should be available electronically through a secure website. You can also control who has access to your proprietary information. In addition, having an electronic version of the operating manual will allow franchisees to quickly notify you of the latest changes in the system. Usually, a manual can contain all relevant information. However, depending on the nature of your business, you can have multiple operation manuals that are tailored to your needs.

Examples of additional manuals include sales brochures, marketing manuals, or technical manuals.

Pre-training Manual

A pre-training manual is used if the time between signing a franchise agreement and opening a franchise store is long, and if the franchisees will be required to perform specific tasks that they may not know. This handbook is awarded to the franchisee when signing the franchise agreement, which should include what the franchisee should know before training.

Among other things, it includes:

- site selection criteria and approval process

- source of financing and instructions on how to obtain financing

- hire key employees if key employees are to be included in the initial training

- establish supplier relationships before opening

- preorder equipment and supplies completed by franchisees.

Franchisees should not be provided with proprietary information until they sign a franchise agreement that includes a non-disclosure agreement.

Required Resources

- operation manual

- pretraining manual

Element 4: Franchisee Training Program

From ancient times to the present, more talents have been trained than geniuses. Inventor king Thomas Edison has a famous saying: Genius is equal to one point of inspiration and ninety-nine points of sweat. After education, these ninety-nine points of sweat can flow in a direction. To operate a business, training is even more important.

Purpose

Training is an important step in granting franchises and is the formal transfer of knowledge required to run a business, including corporate culture and values.

In general, it consists of two parts:

1. Formal classroom training

2. Field training

Who should attend?

Classroom: Franchisees and key personnel

Field: All employees

Where should I train?

Classroom: At the company headquarters

Field: Location of training stores and/or franchisees

Training Period

The initial training of the franchisee and the employees of the business should be as close as possible to the opening time of the franchise store, because it will not be practiced after the study and will soon be forgotten. The training time can be from one week to a maximum of one month depending on the complexity of the business.

Field training is an opportunity to strengthen the four Ps in classroom teaching. When new franchise stores are opened, field training usually ranges from a few days to a month.

Training Materials

Although a separate training manual is applicable, it is important to be consistent with the direction of the operation manual. PowerPoint is not recommended as a training workbook. Other training materials such as work aids, simulations, and other experiential learning techniques are suitable.

Trainer

Initially, the training can be conducted by the founder of the initial store, and later it can be by an expert.

What Should I Teach?

Initially, only the key information can be taught in the classroom. All other information should refer to the operation manual. As franchisees become more aware and familiar with the business, follow-up training and field trips can extend this training.

Required Resources

- development of training courses for franchisees and all positions
- development of training materials
- training leader

Element 5: Franchise Recruitment System

There are many people who have completed their business dreams through franchising, but how to find the suitable franchisee is still open to discussion. Franchise recruitment may be the most concerned topic in franchising. A successful franchise hiring program can increase market share, which is key to any franchise company. Many companies take a casual approach to franchise recruitment, resulting in poor results and great frustration.

In order for a franchise recruitment program to be successful, a franchise recruitment toolbox should have four powerful tools.

1. Strong organisational commitment

2. Powerful franchise recruitment system

3. A great recruiter

4. Maintain a success attitude

Basic Understanding

In many cases, franchisees use the term *sales* as a franchise term that is inaccurate because the franchise is granted to the franchisee.

In essence, franchisees only have the right to operate a franchise within a limited time to provide customers with consistent products, services, and experience in a particular area.

Type of Franchisee

- single store
- multiple shops
- company store
- regional development rights
- replacement of market independent operators
- master license

Franchise Thinking

- Step 1: Create a franchise recruitment system
- Step 2: Recruit target candidate

Step 3: Core story

Step 4: Marketing process

Step 5: Recruitment process

Required Resources

- full-time recruiters

- recruitment collateral

- recruitment website

- recruitment CRM system

- lead generation budget

Element 6: Franchise Support Program

As the saying goes, there is always a woman behind a successful man. In fact, the same is true for a business. It does not mean that there must be a woman behind a man, but there must be a good support behind it. And franchise support includes the following.

Reactive Support

When the franchisee has problems and needs immediate attention.

Active Support

- further strengthen the franchisee's goal

- let franchisees participate in the program

- introduce new products, services, plans, and measures

- continuous improvement of business

- continuous improvement of the skills required for the business

Some support is best provided by the capabilities of the headquarters, whereas other support is best provided through support staff near the franchise site. Therefore when preparing for a franchise, you must plan which ones are supported by the headquarters and which are supported by support personnel near the franchise site.

Required Resources

- support supervisor

- customer relationship management system

- marketing director

- financial officer

- technical director

- product development manager

- support development plan

Element 7: Infrastructure, Technology, and Supply Chain

The last element is the tools needed to operate the business. See the example.

Equipment to Be Provided by the Franchisee

- website
- point of sale system
- supply chain
- provide sales reports to franchisees
- intranet for critical information and secure communications within the franchise ecosystem
- accounting
- sales statistics
- marketing strategy and collateral
- staff training

Equipment to Be Provided by the Franchisor

- website
- franchise recruitment website
- franchise recruitment tools
- social media website
- collection and summary of sales information
- intranet
- supplier relationship management
- innovation

- testing
- training
- customer relationship management
- accounting

At the beginning of the franchise, these devices not only need to be in place, but they also need to be managed continuously. Otherwise, they will hinder the growth of your franchisee or your system.

Franchise financial investment The establishment of a franchise system requires at least the following	Investment description amount

Personnel
 	
    product developer
 	
    recruitment
 	
    principal
 	
    training leader
 	
    marketing manager
 	
    financial manager
 	
    technical director	

Tool	
company website	
franchise website	
intranet	
customer relationship management system	
enterprise sales point intelligence system	
website selection	
investment description amount	
software	
webinar technology	

Resources Required

- franchise agreement
- pretraining manual
- training manual
- recruitment collateral
- generate budget
- total budget investment:

The Role and Responsibility of the Franchisee

The franchisee has two commercial building roles:

1. Establishing your own franchise company

2. Creating a system and helping franchisees build their business.

Once you start a franchise, there are six aspects that you need to think about as a franchisor, and continue to plan and act, so that you will be successful.

1. Create loyal customers

2. Successful franchise recruitment

3. Dedicated training and support

4. Excellent franchise store

5. Effective franchise relationship

6. Strategic business and financial planning

> It's the little things that make the big things possible. Only close attention to the fine details of any operation makes the operation first class.
>
> —John Willard Marriott, founder of the American family-owned company Marriott

Chapter 7

Learn from the International Franchise Winners

> "Concession is a system of doing business. It is very possible to learn from the mistakes of others and benefit from success. Absorbing the success of previous people, cultivating, and paving the way for the seeds of business that they have buried can be thriving."

Franchise Big Winner

Franchising is a business model for success. According to the US Department of Commerce, franchisors have an annual rate of failure of less than 5 per cent. However, for new franchises, success is not automatic, with three requirements: unique products or services, successful track records, and the ability to replicate and teach your business systems. There are three other conditions: the determination, wisdom, and talent to inspire others with their own dreams. Franchising is a system of doing business in which it is very possible to learn from the mistakes of others and benefit from their success.

It is wise to learn from the successful experience of the predecessors and pave the way for the seeds of business that you have buried. The following is a brief and interesting story of some of the big winners of the franchise, to inspire readers. By following examples of successful franchises such as McDonald's, Holiday Inn, Domino's Pizza, Buggy Car Rental, and Sunshine Laundry, franchisors can avoid some of the more common mistakes and get the most out of it. These people have achieved extraordinary success through franchising, and they have made significant contributions to the franchise industry.

The Kingdom of Hamburg

In the mass production of hamburgers, fries, and milkshakes, Ray Kroc became the most famous figure in the franchise. Since he opened his first store in 1955, Ray Kroc's demands for quality, service, cleanliness, and value have become the golden rule of McDonald's. By the time he died in 1984, he had expanded his business into more than 8,000 restaurants worldwide.

As noted in the first chapter, Ray Kroc did not invent franchises, fast food, or McDonald's. What he did was to perfect all three aspects and add his vision to McDonald's.

Ray Kroc began looking for his niche in his early years, and dropped out of school, and opened a music store after his sophomore year. After the war I, Ray Kroc integrated his talent into music and sales. He sold paper cups during the day and played the piano on the radio at night. In the late 1930s, he became fascinated with a multi-purpose blender, and he also developed a blend of five malt and milkshakes. A few years later, the industry's giants introduced a multi-mixer. Ray Kroc did not directly fight against competitors; he instead set the market to change. Education food retailers need more mixers. In 1954, this strategy led him to discover an opportunity to change his life.

After visiting the McDonald's brothers in San Bernardino, Ray Kroc realised that the efficient, low-cost methods used by the brothers were almost perfect and could be easily copied. Although he originally wanted to join their restaurant so that he could sell two or three multi-purpose blenders per new McDonald's, he began to realise that the real benefits could be found in restaurants.

In 1955, Ray Kroc opened his first McDonald's in Des Plaines, and he used it as a demonstration of potential franchisees from the beginning. Two years later, the McDonald's Hamburger booth increased to 37 locations, and by 1959 the franchise store reached 100 stores. By 1961, the number of franchise stores had grown to 228. That year, Ray Kroc acquired shares in McDonald's Brothers for $2.7 million, including the use of their names. In 1969, the 1,000[th] franchise store opened, and it quickly expanded to 2,000 in three years. During this period, McDonald's established its position. By 1980, the total number of McDonald's stores had exceeded 5,000. Ray Kroc understood that the franchise system could only succeed if the franchisees achieved consistent success. That's why Ray Kroc's early focus was on franchisees, not on corporate structures.

Kemmons Wilson Came to the Holiday Inn

In the summer of 1951, Kemmons Wilson took his family for a bad vacation. After returning to Memphis, he vowed to build a motel to eliminate the shortcomings he experienced. The second year, Wilson's first Holiday Inn hotel opened.

He booked a plan for a 120-room large motel instead of the usual 20–25 rooms at the time. The planners who made the plan used their "Holiday Hotel" of the same name as the Bing Crosby movie in 1942. Wilson liked the name and opened his first Holiday Inn hotel in 1952 on one of the main roads to Memphis.

A year and a half after the opening of the first hotel, he longed for the Holiday Inn to become a national chain hotel. His next step was to contact the "most thoughtful person" he knew: Wallace Construction. Together they formed the American Holiday Inn (now Holiday Inns, Inc.) and began franchising these motels. Under their first major push, they invited seventy-five of the nation's leading residential homebuilders to Memphis to market the concept of a Holiday Inn. About sixty builders appeared, and when they heard the franchise advice, almost everyone responded enthusiastically. He saw the beginning of realising his great dreams.

He contacted doctors, lawyers, and other professionals and sold franchises to them. By 1957, fifty franchise stores had opened, and the franchise had been greatly promoted as the interstate highway system began to traverse the country and invited vacationers to take the road. In 1959, the one hundredth franchise store was opened. By 1965, when the Holidex computer reservation system was introduced, the franchise stores had sprung up to more than five hundred. Four years later, the total number exceeded one thousand. Kemmons Wilson was listed by the *Sunday Times of London* as one of the thousand most important men in the twentieth century.

The 1970s was a challenge for Holiday Inn. Although there were more than 1,500 stores in 1973, competitors such as Ramada Inns, Howard Johnson's, and Quality Inn were steadily catching up with the holidays. The oil crisis of 1973 was the most serious blow to Holiday Inn. Lack of fuel has caused many drivers to reduce travel, and the ensuing recession reduced vacations. Holiday Inn's profits and stock prices plummeted, and new growth slowed. The next five years, the company abandoned some uncoordinated acquisitions and gradually stabilised.

After a heart attack in 1979, Kemmons Wilson retired as chairman of the Holiday Inn Group. Looking back, he believes that the honour of Holiday Inn's success must be shared with hundreds of franchisees who have shared some of their dreams over the years. "This is because we have the right people to work for us and ourselves. When they work for themselves, people work harder. I think this is the only way to get the best and best for people."

Managing Domino's Pizza through an Adventure

Over the past twenty-five years, Domino's Pizza has grown from a few university campus pizzerias to global chains with nearly four thousand points of sale. Once upon a time, Tom Monaghan was a member of the St Joseph Boys' Home in Jackson, Michigan. He is now owner of one of the largest and fastest growing fast food chains in the United States.

To raise his tuition fee, Tom Monaghan received a small loan in 1960 to buy a pizzeria near the University of Michigan campus in eastern Michigan.

In the next three years, he began to transform his first pizza restaurant into a simplified operation of Domino's, whose goal is to provide all orders within thirty minutes.

From 1965 to 1968, Domino's had grown to eight stores through franchising and had good sales. The next four years increased the total six times over through the use of franchising. In 1968, the franchise's headquarters, all of the company's records, its principals, and the most sold stores were destroyed in a fire. In the second year, he used the franchise to rapidly expand the number of stores and the number of managers. By 1970, there were 44 Domino's, but there were too many bosses and bureaucrats in the company. Domino's put the company's employees on the most basic essentials, and he let the company re-enter the financial health path. He regained the confidence of the franchisees.

In 1975, the number of Domino's exceeded one hundred and faced some final obstacles before the company's success. Amstar, a manufacturer of Domino's, filed a trademark infringement lawsuit against Domino's. The five-year battle finally succeeded for Domino's, not only strengthening the loyalty of Domino's management but also strengthening the loyalty of franchisees, some of whom used Domino's name for more than fifteen years at the end of the lawsuit.

After the 1980 lawsuit, Domino's total number of agents reached nearly four hundred, of which about 70 per cent were franchisees, and most of which served universities or military towns. The new challenge for Tom Monaghan was to expand into cities and suburbs while maintaining quality and efficiency.

With the continued growth of Domino's Pizza, followed by an average annual growth rate of 45 per cent in six years, company consultants and field representatives visited each store every month, and even twice per month. Any store manager who exceeded the company's current weekly sales record received a Swiss watch worth $15,000 from him as an incentive.

By the beginning of 1987, there were nearly four thousand Domino's, with an average of three new stores opened every day. In the pizza business, only Pizza Hut had more retail stores, and Domino's achieved its goal often thousand stores in the mid-1990s. External expansion was also a top priority, with Domino's stores in Canada, the United Kingdom, Germany, Australia, and Japan. This tremendous success brought him a lot of propaganda and the ability to realise his lifelong dreams.

Budget Rent-A-Car's Jules Lederer

From the 1950s, Jules Lederer built Budget Rent-A-Car into the first nationwide discount car rental chain. Starting with no experience in car rental and franchising, he relied on franchisees to grow the company.

In 1958, Jules Lederer's cousin opened a taxi office in Los Angeles, operating forty-eight used cars, with plans to charge less than Hertz car rentals and Avis car rentals. Using the Avis car rental model as a model, he set a uniform amount of franchise fees and franchise usage schedules, and he limited the percentage of franchisees, which made his company pay a considerable amount of money. For the next two years, Budget Rent-A-Car grew rapidly. By 1962, the company had fifty franchisees across the country. In 1964, there were less than one hundred franchisees in the United States, but four years later, it grew to more than three hundred. In addition, there were about 180 foreign franchisees.

In 1968, eight years after the start of the franchise, the company agreed to exchange stocks across Transamerica Corporation, a financial and insurance company. Jules Lederer made a huge profit from the deal, and he still had a four-year partnership with Budget Rent-A-Car and Transamerica Corporation before the friendship broke up.

Jules Lederer believes that there are three key points that will help Budget Rent-A-Car to succeed, and he believes that any fledgling franchisee can benefit from it. First, there must be an effective, well-defined concept and market research and planning. Second, one must choose franchisees with good qualifications, enthusiasm, and financial resources. "If I grant a franchise to a person who lacks money, and he eventually fails, then the company not only has to pay his fees and taxes, but also damages the company's name and reputation," he said. His third recommendation is to provide training and support. "The relationship between the franchisor and the franchisee is basically a parental relationship," he said. "The franchisee links his trust and money to the franchisor, and in return franchisee must be instructed."

Confucianism Helped Sunshine Laundry

When people are in their early thirties, they are determined to start their own business. Mr Ringo Wong relies on two convictions: not only by his hands, but by mass production. He was not familiar with mass production but chose to join the laundry industry in 1993. He was governed by Confucianism and franchised his business in 2002 to develop a laundry kingdom.

Ringo was educated by his family as a child. He knew that the name of the store should be simple and easy to remember. After growing up, he joined the five-star hotel butler department and received professional training in laundry and clothing care. He was well aware of the entire operation process and laid a solid foundation for him to become the leader in the laundry industry. He decided to start a business and named it Sunshine Laundry.

"Laundry is a traditional family work. As the society progresses, the work of the citizens becomes more and more annoying. Everyday work is from morning to night. When I return home, it is close to 9 pm. It can be said that the work is very exhausting," Ringo said. "I think laundry is too time-consuming. The laundry and hanging time is about 6–7 hours, so people would rather take the clothes out of the street to wash." Mr Wong opened a laundry workshop to serve hard-working citizens.

When he first joined the laundry industry, he opened only the laundry and delivery shop. The clothes were handed over to the dry-cleaning factory. In addition to earning experience, money and time were lost in one year. Finally, he concluded that he could only make profits by setting up his own factory. When he opened his first cottage-style laundry workshop in 1994, he did not know much about the entire workshop, and he did not even understand the administrative management. Later, he seriously consulted the experts and learned from them.

After several efforts, Sunshine Laundry has not been franchised, but there are already five branches. "We teach our employees with traditional Chinese Confucianism to find out where they have done something wrong and learn from the benefits of each other," he said. This set of thinking makes employees happy to work, and thus business is naturally rolling. The laundry workshop has also expanded to four thousand square metres.

After opening the eighth branch in 2001, the market competition became fierce. He believed that it was necessary to speed up the pace of opening branches. However, the funds were always limited, and so he decided to create his own franchise. At first he took inspiration through books, surfing the Internet, and referring to existing franchisees. It took a year to figure out, but he was still worried about how to get started. In another case of seeking expert help, Ringo met a company that specialised in designing franchises for SMEs. In the end, in 2002 Ringo first got five franchisees to join, and in 2003 there were eight new franchisees.

In order to make the franchisee profitable, Ringo spent two years writing seven management workbooks for training purposes. He had an idea in his mind. "The laundry industry is a very professional industry, from the understanding of fabrics, chemical treatment usage and maintenance of various machines, knowledge of picking, ironing, service and management, leather care, industrial safety, etc. It takes at least three years to complete the preparation of a laundry apprentice. All of the above shows the profession of the laundry industry." In addition, he introduced the laundry equipment staging plan in 2009, which let the franchisees reduce costs and made them more profitable.

The increase in branches and franchisees meant that business was also increasing, and the rental cost and salaries on human resources rose sharply. He had an idea. "Since the rent has been paid, can it be changed to twenty-four hours?" With such thoughts in mind, Ringo immediately worked on the study on the location of the store and adopted the payment service of electronic money in 2007. Office workers welcomed such policy. By 2018, twenty-two of the forty-four branches in Hong Kong had been converted into twenty-four-hour, self-service laundry, which is also the mainstream model for the future of Sunshine Laundry.

Chapter 8

Franchise Law in Hong Kong

"Most franchise laws are the gospel of franchisees, and adherence to these laws can enhance the reputation of franchisees and ensure the safety of franchisees."

Franchising and Law

Hong Kong has a sound legal system, but there is no special franchise law. What should be done in the face of disputes? To be frank, there is no need to worry. Disputes arising from franchise agreements in Hong Kong are governed by common law (especially the principles of contract law) and laws relating to registration, authorisation, and intellectual property protection, including the Trade Marks Ordinance, the Copyright Ordinance, the Registered Designs Ordinance, and the Patents Ordinance. Although there are no relevant laws and regulations in Hong Kong, you can also refer to the example of the US Franchise Law, which is also beneficial to readers of the future development of the franchise business. In 1971, in response to increasing legal violations in franchising, the state of California issued the first national law specifically for franchise registration. Throughout the 1970s and early 1980s, other states followed suit, and fourteen of them (and Alberta, Canada) had rules and regulations that required franchisees to provide extensive information about the nature of franchise products. Before the franchise is offered and sold, the history of the franchisee is presented. This process is often referred to as registration, and the fourteen states that need to be registered are referred to in the industry as registered states.

There are some important topics in it.:

Maintenance and repair. Franchise agreements often ignore a clause that requires franchisees to maintain their stores to a certain minimum standard as specified in the operating manual. If the franchisee does not do so, the clause may allow the franchisor to perform the necessary repairs at the expense of the franchisee. It may also include funds consisting of regular contributions from franchisees for refurbishment of franchisees.

Insurance. Many agreements have little or no mention of insurance terms. The franchise agreement should require the franchisee to bear at least the worker's compensation and property insurance liability, and to stipulate the minimum coverage. The franchisee should receive a copy of the policy and any cancellation notice as a co-insurant. The franchisee may wish to recommend an insurance company, but the franchisee has the right to choose its own underwriter as long as the policy meets the franchisee's insurance coverage requirements. In addition, if the franchisee does not receive appropriate protection, the franchisor can take the initiative to insure and BE immediately reimbursed by the franchisee.

Training. The training of the franchisee is the final stage of the franchise. The agreement stipulates that the franchisee must successfully complete the training. If this is not the case, it is important that the franchisor can terminate the franchise agreement and retain a certain percentage of the franchise fee.

Advertising. The franchise agreement should require the franchisee to use the advertising materials developed or approved by the franchisor and clearly state how to submit the materials for approval. Many franchisors require franchisees to provide advertising funds that benefit in common to all franchisees managed by them, and the agreement should specify to whom the fee should be paid and the amount of the fee.

Interest transferability. If the franchisee wishes to sell its franchise, the terms of the agreement shall specify the terms that can be implemented, including the following.

1. The franchisor provides training to the franchisee

2. The franchisee successfully completes the training

3. The franchisee pays transfer and training fees to the franchisor

4. The franchisee pays all fees in advance to the franchisor

The agreement should indicate that the franchisor will not unreasonably reject the franchisee and may give the franchisee the right to purchase the franchise first. Finally, the agreement should stipulate that if the franchisee dies, the franchisor can operate or sell the business, and under what conditions the franchisor can obtain the franchise.

All of the issues mentioned above should be discussed with a lawyer. But even if you are fortunate enough to find a lawyer with extensive experience in dealing with franchising, you should not expect him to make business decisions for you alone. Want to continue renting? Like everyone else, this decision will be based on financial capabilities, the importance of location to business concepts, the degree of control over franchisees, and other non-legal factors.

Finally, it is recommended that the franchisor be prepared to face litigation on the day the franchise agreement is signed. This sounds cynical, but in today's business environment, warnings are effective as more and more reliance on litigation. The franchisor should carefully record everything that the franchisee has done and maintain a comprehensive set of documents and records to show each call, every dispute that has been resolved, every visit to the franchise, and each franchisee not following the rules. Of course, if the franchisee does not follow the rules, it should be notified immediately, otherwise the rules may not be enforced in the future.

Frequently Asked Questions

Even after studying various state laws, many franchisors have raised specific questions about the interpretation and daily impact of numerous laws. Based on experience, the following are common questions about franchising.

1. Can I ask the franchisee to buy products from me?

Usually not, but there are exceptions. One key point is that in the United States, franchisors can ask franchisees to buy products of a certain quality without actually selling them to franchisees. For example, KFC requires franchisees to purchase a "secure mixture of herbs and spices" from a designated distributor.

The franchisor alleged that the franchisee used its power to force the franchisee to purchase products from them, which was called a bundling case. The court has ruled that certain tying requirements in the relationship between the franchisor and the franchisee violate the competition law. However, the courts have recognised that the nature of franchising may apply to situations where the products and services that are purchased do not constitute an illegal relationship. Illegal contact occurs when a franchisor asks a franchisee to purchase a second product to be allowed to purchase the franchisor's main product. For example, many oil companies used to supply gasoline to service stations that buy tires, batteries, and other accessories. After these cases appeared in the 1950s and 1960s, this practice was found illegal in the competition bill.

2. How do I answer how much franchisees can earn from my franchise?

As we said, the penalty for misrepresentation can be serious, and so I strongly discourage the franchisor from making any misrepresentation of marketing. In the past, some franchisors showed a piece of paper to franchisees with a chart showing that franchisees would earn $50,000 when sales were $300,000, $100,000 when sales were $500,000, and $150,000 when sales were $700,000, but in fact no franchisees are operational, or only a few franchisees have sales close to $200,000. The legislature's response is to develop specific claims guidelines for income based on sound financial standards.

Each legal guide contains a statement of how to provide franchisees with actual or projected sales, profits, or revenue. Therefore if you fail to tell your franchisees what your future income may be, you may not need to make such a statement to avoid promises to the franchisees the expected future earnings. If the franchisee's income does not meet the commitment conditions, your worst consequences may be in the face of legal proceedings from the franchisee.

3. Can I prevent my franchisee from doing business elsewhere?

Franchisors cannot prevent franchisees from selling goods and services to consumers in their stores. However, if the franchisee does not conduct business within the scope of the agreement, then you can limit the franchisee to continue the promotion, and you have the right to ask the franchisee to compensate for the sales generated in the franchise scope of the agreement.

A more effective way is to leave the franchisee in the designated area and formulate specific implementation plans for the area, such as the annual sales that the franchisee must complete each month. Under the concept of primary responsibility, the court considered that the above activities could be enforced.

4. Can I limit the price that the franchisee collects from the customer?

No. The court found this pricing to be a violation of competition law. What you can do at most is to recommend your franchisee the price of the goods or services you sell. However, franchisees may get franchisors to agree to participate in special regional or nationwide promotions to provide products or services at a special standard price.

5. Can I sell goods and services to different franchisees at different prices?

No, unless it involves factors such as delivery costs or purchase quantities. These must also apply to all franchisees.

6. Can I compete with my franchisee in the same field?

There are only two cases: first, when your franchisee has not been granted any exclusive location, and second, when you have not caused any financial damage to your franchisee. Due to the exclusive location arrangement, the franchisee has the right to open an exclusive franchise in a particular area stated on the contract. Most of the exclusive location franchise arrangements now cover only a few miles of radius in a big city. Since 1969, McDonald's has restricted most exclusive location franchises to certain street addresses.

7. Can I terminate a franchisee who does not comply with my designated business and continues to operate?

Yes, but to be within reasonable limits. You must take appropriate action to do so, and in order to reduce the threat of litigation, these reasons should be clearly stated in the franchise agreement and operating manual. McDonald's successfully terminated a franchisee in Paris in 1982 after repeatedly informing a restaurant that it had not met its cleanliness standards. The franchise may be terminated after giving sufficient time to correct the violation. With the support of McDonald's, this termination was strongly supported by the court.

Sometimes if the franchisee claims that it responds slightly to the local market's professional skills, it makes a slight change in business hours, or it changes the restaurant menu to suit the neighbour's eating habits, without considering most of the restaurant customers. At the time of religion and eating habits, the court may then look at whether the franchisee's requirements are reasonable or appropriate to local market changes.

8. Can I prevent my franchisee from cancelling his franchise a few years later and use my system to run the business without paying?

In the United States, this depends on the type of state and franchise program the franchisee is in. For commercial forms of franchising, there are restrictive clauses in the legal documents at the beginning of the "limitation" and "late restriction" sections to prevent franchisees from operating similar businesses for a certain period of time within a specific geographical area. Execution varies from state to state. For example, some states in the United States are reasonably preventing franchisees from engaging in this business within twenty-five miles and within two years. Other states require fewer restrictions to make the contract enforceable.

9. When can I legally provide franchisee franchises?

To provide franchisee franchise rights, you must first establish a proper franchise agreement and provide the above notice. Depending on the location of your company and the location of your franchisee and the location of the sale, you may also need to register the franchise in the appropriate state. You must provide a copy of the issuance circular to each franchisee at the first face-to-face meeting, at which the franchise is discussed. Even then, you must wait at least ten business days before accepting any money and before executing a franchise or related agreement. The agreement must be completed within five working days before the franchise is accepted.

10. Can I sell the franchise to different people at different fees?

Yes. You can charge a lower franchise fee to someone who knows your business, and a full-time novice who needs extensive training will be charged a higher fee. When developing a franchise plan, you can also declare that you intend to sell a certain amount of franchise at an introductory price and indicate that you intend to raise the price after a certain date or a certain number of franchises are sold. In other cases, you may sell multiple outlets at once and offer discounts to buy multiple outlets or larger areas. However, the key is that all potential buyers must have the same opportunity under the same conditions to purchase the franchise at that price.

Finally, legal issues should not dominate your decision-making process. Don't let the law decide whether you grant a franchise. This is a business decision and must be based on the various criteria we discussed in the previous chapters. However, most franchise laws are the gospel of franchisees, and adherence to these laws can enhance the reputation of franchises and ensure the safety of franchisees.

Chapter 9

Franchise System Development Time Schedule and Financial Investment

> "It takes money to make money, and few companies can carry out franchises without a certain financing channel."

William Somerset Maugham cautiously states, "Money is like the sixth sense—without it, you can't use the other five." You can't start a franchise without money. However, the question is not whether there is funding for expansion, but whether it has the ability to raise additional capital when needed.

Franchising is a lucrative business, but as the saying goes, making money requires money. Few companies are able to carry out franchise without a certain financing channel, whether through bank loans, private equity offerings, or some kind of venture capital arrangement. Despite the enviable franchise performance, the financial institution does not seem to be eager to help successful companies become franchisees. Part of the problem is banks, investment brokerage firms, and other financial institutions lack enough knowledge about franchising and its potential. This chapter is helpful for franchisees and financial professionals, especially to explain their financing options to franchisees.

How Much Do I Need?

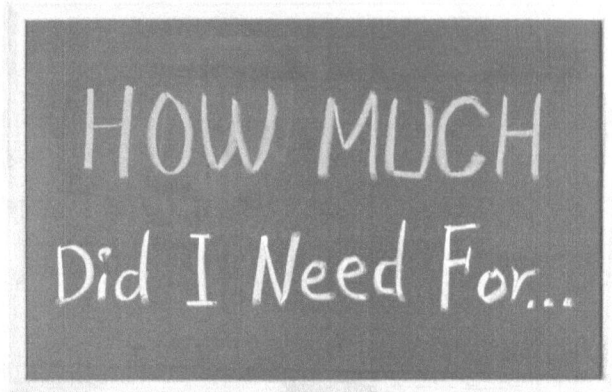

Franchising is developed in stages, and it is a way of expanding. Creating a business that can succeed is a prerequisite for franchising. Many entrepreneurs get some form of financing in the form of personal loans through friends, family, or banks. However, more and more people today are using an easier way to get capital and start business. They refinanced after establishing equity.

The second phase of development is venture capital. Venture capital refers to a new type of financing method for financing high-tech enterprises or venture capital entrepreneurs.

The two main questions about franchising and the problems faced by new franchisor are "How much does franchising cost?" and "Where will franchising get?" Two other questions: "How much money can I start a business without a loan?" and "If you decide to seek financing, what should be used as collateral?"

Every franchise is basically service oriented, and unless your business involves a large amount of real estate ownership or high-priced goods transactions, there may not be enough collateral to provide the bank in exchange for the required funds. If you are too optimistic, you may mistakenly assess the time it takes to make a profit. This is a common failure, especially in companies with poor performance. If your business is between the ages of five and ten years, you may experience some ups and downs and be able to incorporate both into your predictions. If your business is relatively new and has not experienced anything other than success, you might assume that success can be transferred to your franchise project in the same amount of time. The keyword for proper evaluation is time. Your predictions may be conservative, but you must consider that your goal will cost you more money than you think; it is far better than borrowing too little.

If you underestimate the time required, you will run out of money until you reach your goal. If this happens, you may need to change your plan to avoid affecting your ability to borrow and eventually lose your business. Before you borrow money, listen to the opinions of the experts you trust, do everything in your power to accurately assess your needs, and take a firm and calm look at your business and future management factors.

How Do I Get It?

Most banks will be happy to fund you and set interest rates that will benefit them.

Commercial Banks

Are commercial banks a suitable target for your loans, or will you waste your time? Usually banks need a lot of collateral before offering commercial loans. Unless your company is fully capitalised by its own cash reserves, existing cash flow, or other private funds, it is difficult to obtain a bank for the border cost of the franchise plan. When banks look at your balance sheet and company valuations, they tend to discount the main assets of your business: the knowledge, experience, and capabilities of you and your employees.

Banks are asset-based money lenders. Despite this trend across the banking sector, some banks are aware of the potential of franchising. For example, ten banks in the UK and five banks in Canada have developed franchise financing options. The Royal Bank of Canada has provided more than

$400 million in financing options to franchisors and franchisees. In the United States, citizens of Atlanta and the National Bank of the South established a franchise corporate finance department.

If you are looking for a bank loan, you must convince the banker that the market for your goods or services is growing, not falling. To do this, market data and reliable business forecasts should be used to support your business. You can even help your career by increasing the banker's knowledge of franchising, but the banker's decision-making is based on intuition, and you must reach out to bankers in a knowledgeable, responsible, and cordial manner. You can write the best business plan in the world, but if the banker doesn't like you, please check out somewhere else. Don't think that everything is taken for granted. The conditions of the bank often change. Last year's bull market could become a bear market this year.

By the way, no matter where you go, the more complex the concept, the better. A business plan with detailed, comprehensive forecasts is worth the time and money to complete in preparation.

Equity Financing

Bank loans are essentially debt financing, and the money you borrow needs to be repaid. After assessing funding needs, another option to consider is equity financing. In this case, you are not looking for a lender but an investor; he or she will provide you with the funds in exchange for the company's future earnings.

According to experience, most entrepreneurs tend to seek equity-based financing when launching franchise plans. In fact, most successful entrepreneurs will soon seek equity financing through private or public offerings, and a few companies succeed in family offices. The problem of equity financing in most companies is not whether it should be, but when. If you are just developing a franchise plan, you can consider seeking equity financing; if you release 25 per cent of the shares to investors in the process, then you can get 25 per cent of the funds from investors; when you want to get more money, you may try to sell more shares. Be careful not to oversell the shares so as to not lose control of the company. You can sell the original shares to your friends and relatives for funding at the seed stage of the project, and then you can turn to find banker loans when you decide to add additional capital. Finally, when your concept has been proven with a strong growth model, look for equity financing.

The most common form of equity financing is through the issuance of stocks. Initial public offerings (IPOs) are usually issued by companies seeking two million US dollars or more and are discussed in more detail later in this chapter. At the same time, you can also issue shares without listing. For example, you can sell your company's shares to a limited number of buyers through an investment bank that provides private equity financing services directly to investors, and you can set a certain dollar limit on the number of shares sold.

As the plan grows, you should wait until your franchise plan is successfully implemented and then seek equity financing. At this point, when you have 20 to 100 stores running, your business plan may need $2–20 million or more to build more direct stores in key markets—not just to generate additional franchise sales, but to train and supervise the management of flagship employees. At this time, your company will show a higher value than before. Past franchise and renewal fees, as well as sales or rental of products, services, and real estate to franchisees, can be used to predict future earnings. Now, in order to get the money you need to accelerate your franchise development plan, you can decide to use equity capital or IPO for equity financing.

Venture Capital

More than six hundred venture capital firms in the United States provide private investment capital to companies that cannot obtain capital from traditional sources. Venture capital firms usually check hundreds of potential investments before making a deal.

Typically, a venture capital group will value the company and predict its earnings over a five- to seven-year period, as well as preparing detailed financial projections, including a three- to five-year capital demand analysis with time spent on capital investment, what the debt is, the rate of return, and the internal rate of return. This analysis is submitted to the business owner and, if the parties reach an agreement, provide funds in exchange for the notes and choose to participate in the company's ownership. Venture capitalists ensure their investment through stock equity; the amount depends on the level of risk, but it is also possible that some loans will be referred to third-party lenders on an asset-based basis. Note that if the borrower does not meet expectations of the return, the venture capital firm has the right to intervene and control the company through stock ownership, and you may eventually lose control of the company.

If you choose the right venture capital firm, it can be a valuable partner because it can not only help the debt but also help and advise by matching some of its investment with the lending funds of the affiliated banks. The company can help hire qualified managers to get financing for franchisors.

Some franchisors combine venture capital with initial public offerings. In the first private placement, the venture capitalist obtained the warrant or option, and the price of the additional stock purchased at the time of the company's listing was lower than the market price on the initial public offering date. When providing the second round of stocks, the value of the company and the value of the stock should increase. From the perspective of venture capitalists, this strategy can effectively obtain funds from the company and invest the funds of other investors. To do this, it usually requires the assistance of an investment bank and an audit firm because the company needs a three-year audited audit statement. Of course, you may be fortunate enough to find an angel investor to fund you without having to apply for public offerings to raise funds.

Initial Public Offering

The first thing to understand is that IPOs are not used to raise hundreds of thousands of dollars, but rather cost a lot of legal and accounting fees and printing and distribution services.

Listing is the sale of a portion of your company's stock to a large number of investors to get the cash you need so that the company can reach its full potential. To do this, you need to convince the securities underwriters (brokers or investment banking companies) that your company has sufficient strength and good prospects to prove the correctness of the listing. The job of a securities underwriter is to determine the value of your company and then sell the number of shares you decide to issue to the public.

One of the keys to a successful issuance is to choose the right securities underwriter, a reputable company, and a large number of regulated investors. But choosing a securities underwriter is only part of the listing. You want to make your company's valuation as high as possible and sell it in the necessary percentage range to get the money you need. The goal of securities underwriters is to sell their stocks to convince their investors that the value of these stocks will soon appreciate. The easiest way for an insurance company to achieve this goal is to set a low price for your company to rise immediately after the stock price is issued. One of the ways to evaluate is to gain insight into how the insurer evaluated the company and apply it rigorously to its own company. Another way is to find an experienced financial consultant who understands the underwriting skills and will negotiate on your behalf.

Franchisors are not the only companies that need funds—franchisees need them. Franchisees usually need money to buy franchises and pay for rent, equipment, and working capital. After that, franchisees need funds to build more branches. In order to obtain funding, franchisees can use the same options as franchisors, refinancing individual holdings and applying for traditional bank loans.

The healthy development of franchising is inseparable from the strong support and cooperation of financial institutions. In order to speed up the enthusiasm of mobilising China's huge social capital, the State Council executive adopted the "Management Measures for Infrastructure and Public Utilities Franchising" and clearly stated that the state encourages financial institutions to provide financial advisors and financing consultants for franchise projects and financial services such as syndicated loans. Policy-oriented and development-oriented financial institutions can provide differentiated credit support for franchise projects. For eligible projects, the loan period can be up to thirty years. You may explore the use of franchise project to expect the income pledge loans to support the use of related income as a source of repayment.

The "Management Measures for Infrastructure and Public Utilities Franchising" also encourages the establishment of industrial funds and other forms of shares to provide franchise project capital, and it encourages franchise project companies to carry out structured financing, issue project income notes and asset support bills. This encourages franchise projects to expand the financing channels by establishing private equity funds, introducing strategic investors, issuing corporate bonds, and projecting income bonds, corporate bonds, and non-financial corporate bond financing instruments. In addition, the "Management Measures for Infrastructure and Public Utilities Franchising" strengthened the support of government investment. Relevant departments of the people's government at or above the county level may explore the establishment of infrastructure and public utility franchise guidance funds with financial institutions, and they can support the construction and operation of franchise projects through different means such as investment subsidies, financial subsidies, and loan interest subsidies.

Second, the core of franchising is the agreement between the government and the society, sharing risks, long-term cooperation, and the strength of each exhibition to jointly provide quality public goods and services. In this sense, government integrity is essential. Franchise projects often involve large amounts of investment, long periods of time, and multiple stakeholders, and they are related to relevant government departments and some intermediaries. Therefore the government needs long-term stable and predictable cooperation and support mechanisms.

All in all, franchisors have a variety of ways to finance, but keep in mind that financing is like buying a business concept from someone else. The key is to set a price that someone is willing to pay and that is reasonable.

Chapter 10

Go International

> "The US Department of Commerce says franchising is a 'wave of the future' and has grown into one of the most visible and open business forms in existence."

In 2015, the sales of China's top 100 franchise companies reached 434.5 billion yuan. The franchise top 100 has 128,000 chain stores, of which 106,000 are franchise stores, each with an average of 1,280 chain stores. In 2015, the number of franchise stores and the total number of stores franchising 100 companies increased by 14 per cent and 11 per cent, respectively. Franchising is still the most interesting entrepreneurial model for investors and the best choice for the rapid development of franchising.

Who knows where the positive expansion of franchising will develop?

Trends in Franchising

Hotel industry. On a global scale, most hotel operators have struck a balance between franchise hotels and commissioned hotels. It is estimated that two-thirds are franchise operations and one-third are entrusted management. However, the franchise model has become more and more popular and has become a trend in the hospitality industry. The concept of consumer upgrades in the new era has always been obvious, and consumer demand for hotels has changed. With the importance of needs such as convenience, hygiene, and safety, consumers are more willing to choose the hotels that they like and that can represent them emotionally. For example, since the establishment of the 7 Days Ronghe Hotel operated in China in 2005, after nine years of rapid development, the total number of branches has exceeded 2,000, covering 300 cities nationwide and becoming the first brand of China's economy hotel.

Retail industry. As traditional retailers struggle to launch e-commerce and mobile Internet on international franchise networks, they are increasingly connected. For example, at the end of September 2017, Chow Tai Fook Jewellery had 2,358 jewellery sales outlets in mainland China, 39 per cent of which were operated by franchisees. Chow Tai Fook Official Mall is the official e-commerce platform of Chow Tai Fook Jewellery Group. It was officially launched on 1 October 2011 and is dedicated to providing customers with a new and reliable online shopping experience for jewellery. The official mall offers unique member point value-added services and product security code verification services.

Health care industry. The global healthcare industry has a total value of 3.72 trillion. People's attention to healthy living has increased. A large number of fitness companies operating under the franchise model have emerged around the world. Anytime Fitness, a franchise chain from the United States, is optimistic about the Hong Kong market and believes that the franchise model will help open up new markets. It was founded in 2002 and features twenty-four-hour operations. For busy working populations, irregular work schedules are very common. The twenty-four-hour fitness centre is a viable business model in Hong Kong. The Anytime Fitness franchise store currently has more than 3,000 stores worldwide, and it took only 11 years to open the first batch of 2,000 franchise stores.

Catering industry. Exploring the road of mutual benefit through franchising specialisation, branding, and capitalisation is a useful attempt to break the profit bottleneck of chain restaurants. However, in the franchise process, how to avoid damage to the brand image should be the focus of the catering industry. Under the trend of economic globalisation, China has become the largest developing country. Some well-known foreign brands, such as KFC and McDonald's, have been introduced to China. The unique Western food culture brings people new choices. McDonald's previously announced that its strategic cooperation with CITIC, CITIC Capital, and Carlyle Group has been successfully completed. The strategic cooperation has been approved by the relevant Chinese regulatory authorities and officially completed on 31 July 2017. The new company, Golden Arch (China) Co., Ltd., will become McDonald's largest franchise outside the United States, managing approximately 2,500 McDonald's restaurants in mainland China and Hong Kong with approximately 240 McDonald's restaurants.

Service industry. In the service industry, multi-brand franchising has a growing trend. In 2015, the franchise industry in the Philippines was dominated by American brands, and the number of US companies operating service hotline centres increased rapidly, enabling Filipinos to accept twenty-four-hour shift work patterns, thereby promoting the growth of franchise companies such as housekeeping services, laundry, and home service. Twenty-four-hour shifts help meet the needs of business process outsourcing.

How Does Franchising Take the Road of the Future?

International franchise brands are accelerating in opening up, and domestic franchise brands are favoured. Domestic and foreign franchise groups have promoted the franchise model as an expansion strategy, business model, organisational system, and service model, and that has created new opportunities. However, the Chinese franchise market also has extremely distinctive features. Even domestic chain brands that have achieved franchise success in terms of volume expansion still face challenges, and the franchise model is a necessary condition for innovation.

- Raise the franchise to the strategic development of the company.

    From the case of several large chain hotel groups in China, the corresponding real estate developers have become an important interest-binding relationship. Therefore in order to adapt to the company's future development, franchisors must pay attention to the franchise model and the service and management of real estate developers, and promote it to the company's strategic development. The franchisor should start from the corporate philosophy and corporate vision, increase the concept of "serving the enterprise, realising consumer value", and provide professional services around the consumer needs at the enterprise level and system level. China's hotel management group has added "becoming a franchise service provider" in its vision, highlighting the company's emphasis on consumer interests.

    People demand food every day, and the catering industry's operating threshold is lower than that of other industries. Hong Kong's Mian Cafe and Mian Cafe in China are the two leisure restaurant brands of Zhongsi Group. Founded in 1997, the group is mainly engaged in Japanese and Taiwanese style noodles and pearl milk tea. In 1999, it began to adopt the franchise business model development and created the brand in Hong Kong. The highest decision-making and management of the Mian Cafe Restaurant, including the founder Mr.Chan and Mrs.Chan and the founder Mr Li, laid the foundation for the franchise in internal management. They jointly formulated the company's major decisions, including brand strategy, brand development, and promotion such as strategy, electronic marketing, and other services.

- Respond to consumer needs and pay attention to the top-level design structure.

The strategy determines the structure, and the structure follows the strategy. If the franchise is elevated to a strategic level, it means that all consumers will become strategic users and then transform the internal organisational structure, staffing, management systems, business processes, and even corporate culture into a franchise model. This change will bring a devastating future. Top design should have a global perspective. China is now the world's largest economic power. China's problems are also global issues. The issues that need to be addressed in the top-level design are often major global issues that are closely related to the development of the world economy and will affect the world's investment, consumption, and trade. Similarly, policies and strategies to address these issues must also consider international interests and possible changes in the international environment. The top-level design is to solve macro and systemic problems, and the franchisee must combine the grassroots exploration, breakthrough, and trial-and-error pioneering spirit. The 365 Hotel has gradually turned to this structure, and the organisational structure of the entire company has been transformed into a franchise-based structure. At present, the 365 Hotel has spread to Hebei, Henan, Shandong, Shanxi, Beijing, Tianjin, Liaoning, Heilongjiang, and other provinces and cities. The total size of stores has reached more than

260. Based on the customer's consumption power, the 365 Hotel launched a light franchise model, 365+ Yunmeng Hotel, which optimises the franchisee's one-stop service model and internal accountability mechanism for the single business hotel hardware facilities standard, and which quickly resolves the franchise business difficulties encountered, regional supervision, and even resident support to solve the three difficulties of a single hotel: no unified brand, no unified membership system, and no unified appointment channels.

- Form a strong alliance with the franchise platform.

The Asia Branding and Franchising Association focuses on a number of well-known local and international brands. The Asia Branding and Franchising Association was founded in June 2014, and more than a hundred of franchisors and individual brand companies have joined so far. The association aims to bring successful entrepreneurs together on the international stage of Hong Kong. Through cross-generation, cross-industry, and cross-city exchanges, franchisors will demonstrate their determination to promote corporate sustainability and make the brand stand out internationally. Since its inception, the Asia Branding and Franchising Association has always adhered to the philosophy of "integrity service, customer first, entrepreneurial success, and wholehearted service to franchisees". On the one hand, the association will showcase the latest franchise brands, enabling entrepreneurs and investors to access the latest business opportunities faster. On the other hand, it also works with a wide range of media to attract the most demanding investors, enabling investment companies to establish their own channels in the shortest possible time.

The Asia Branding and Franchising Association provides practical and reliable business opportunity information to build a rich and diverse platform for entrepreneurial information. After four years of hard work, it has completed many fruitful modifications and upgrades, from website design, function development and brand promotion to social networks such as Facebook, Instagram, and more. As the founder of Hong Kong's local brand, B.Duck, Eddie Hui is also the vice president of the Asia Branding and Franchising Association. In 2005, B.Duck was very popular in Hong Kong with a cute appearance. Later, with good products, it entered the China's market through good event marketing, becoming the second largest independent IP in China, and then it happened in Japan. Japanese people loved the brand. After being developed for twelve years, it also succeeded in making the brand franchise with this momentum, without additional financing, and accumulated a large amount of funds. Twelve years ago, Eddie hoped to send a toy to his children and accompany the children to take a bath. This has become the brand concept of B.Duck. Its success is to develop the product with care. In 2013, China advocated "One Belt, One Road" and brought the cultural industry to South East Asia. Regardless of the government's resources and the support of the business community, B.Duck can cooperate with the national policy to expand the brand's power map to South East Asia such as South Korea, Thailand, and Malaysia, and even as far as South America, gradually copying the steps of successful franchising in Japan, from the pop-up store to the physical store and finally into a franchise. China emphasises IP development. B.Duck currently has eight offices, one of which is in Huizhou. It can enjoy the local policy concessions of the Huizhou government. The first development model is to export to Japan, then Thailand and South Korea, and then back to China. Quickly copying the franchise in China and breaking the previous model of self-established managers' employment and warehouses in direct-operated stores, B.Duck instead sent representatives from one province to the city, looking for agents to sell the trademarks to local franchisees, and then it applied them to shoes and the clothes. Developing IP is like creating a star: it needs a long period of time. At the same time, there must be a concept behind it. The current fans of B.Duck are girls, students, mothers, and children, which consists of different age groups. Eddie also puts B.Duck into animation series to cater to the children's market, like Hello Kitty, which has the theme products before the launch of cartoon film. B.Duck also has the same theme catering service and theme park. Each place has authorisation. There are many different teams in the country to operate, and so B.Duck's brand has developed into the image of the public. In the end, Eddie believes that persistence is the most important. At the peak period, B.Duck has offices in the first-tier cities of China, such as Beijing, Shanghai, Guangzhou, Shenzhen, Zhongqing, and WuHan, but it still hasn't lost its direction because of rapid success. B.Duck continues to seek the right brand elements and maintains the growth with tens of millions of online media fans.

- Establish a franchise service system around the needs of technology.

In today's hotel industry, competition is getting more and more intense. More and more managers want to introduce IT technology to provide hotel guests with a better service experience while improving employee productivity, thereby controlling and reducing hotel operating costs. Based on these challenges, the 365 Hotel has proposed the following requirements: external unified number service, information record archiving, intelligent pre-dial function, and knowledge base sharing. After applying the call centre system, the business volume of the 365 Hotel has increased significantly. At present, the scale is about a dozen seats. Once the recorded full service call has been fully recorded, the hotel can view the service date, service staff, guest number, service hours, and more. Through background data analysis and reporting, managers can accurately grasp the various data of the system. For example, based on the volume of queries, the 365 Hotel can determine the hotel's active service highlights, provide personalised service to customers, respond quickly to customer needs, solve problems in a closed loop, improve customer satisfaction, and use IT to achieve hotel process reengineering to improve effectiveness.

The Future Challenge of Franchising

Many franchisees have realised that the impact of e-commerce and the entry of international brands into the new era of information channels have become the biggest challenge they face, thus breaking the information asymmetry and making consumers more accustomed to franchisees than ever before. Business change has become a crucial future issue.

- The market segment needs to be better.

    McDonald's corporate philosophy is QSCV—namely, quality, service, cleanliness, and value. **Quality:** The quality management of McDonald's is very strict. After the food is produced, it will be discarded after a period of time. **Services:** This includes the quick and comfortable feeling of the store building, the setting of business hours, the service attitude of the sales staff, and more. **Cleaning:** McDonald's requires employees to stay clean and establish a good, clean image. **Value:** This conveys the concept of McDonald's "providing customers with more valuable high-quality products". In 1955, McDonald's opened its first model store in north-eastern Chicago and established a strict operating system, the QSCV operating system, which is quality, service, cleanliness, and value. With this business model, McDonald's has implemented a second-generation franchise. The quality of spices, meat, and vegetables used by all McDonald's in the world is set by the company. The production process has also been completed; each new product has a set of regulations. McDonald's relies on this type of business to make it grow rapidly. According to the plan announced by McDonald's, by the end of 2018, the proportion of franchise stores in the total number of company stores will increase from the current 81 per cent to 90 per cent. This will save the company $300 million in annual management fees. McDonald's has adopted the development of the industry and made great efforts in market segmentation. The era of McDonald's gradually improving its operation is coming.

In Hong Kong, finding a comfortable home is the wish of everyone. The real estate industry is therefore hitting the market. Century 21 entered the Hong Kong market in 1994 and introduced the franchise of real estate shops. In 2013, in conjunction with the population policy development of the 9 Dawan Districts of the Belt and Road, in some new infrastructure cities such as Hengqin, Zhongshan, Zhuhai, and Macau, some new service stores have been added. Century 21 provides the Hong Kong people with the latest information on real estate, and this kind of convenience is not available in small- and medium-sized individual stores. Century 21 provides professional services, which is their core value. Because of the close contact with domestic developers as sales channels, Century 21 as a middleman to help sales will also complement the franchisees. The problem in Hong Kong is the issue of population policy rather than a problem of land. The property market in Hong Kong has thirteen trillion inventories in real estate. An average of 57,400 new immigrants from the mainland come to Hong Kong each year, all of which are mainly domestically level professionals. When the real estate in some cities in China is banned, they can pay 30 per cent more to purchase Hong Kong real estate. Therefore the development of Century 21 in the form of a franchise is absolutely beneficial. The purpose of Century 21 is to set up a home for Hong Kong customers here for the first time to perfect their living conditions. Century 21 will specifically teach real estate agents more knowledge, because each district has precautions for buying a building, which can provide franchisees with more local policies and knowledge growth in other domestic urban areas, o that franchisees can easily develop their business. With $15 billion in commission, it allows franchisees to enjoy the profits of the entire real estate market, in which the development is not inferior compared to other franchise industries.

- Encounter a crisis of change and seek a more localised way of survival.

The turnover of a single store declined. The difficulty of selecting a new store and the talent gap are still two major problems that plague the development of franchise. When foreign-funded hotels entered the Chinese market for the first time, they seized the dual benefits of national policies and market welfare, and they formed the management model of Chinese owners and foreign management teams. With the rise of state capital and changes in consumption structure, the advantages of international hotels have gradually disappeared. According to Changjiang Securities survey data, the proportion of foreign-invested enterprises has dropped from around 4 per cent in 2004 to around 2 per cent in 2016, and the market share has shrunk by half. In the face of the crisis of change, foreign hotels began to seek a more localised way of survival. Many foreign brands choose to rely on Chinese partners to expand their territory, which is actually another franchise model. In May 2016, InterContinental Hotels announced the opening of a franchise for Crowne Plaza Hotels; in November 2017, it announced that it will open a franchise model for Crowne Plaza Hotels and Resorts in China. Under the franchise model, hotel owners can organise teams to manage and own all the intellectual property behind the brand.

- Seize the capital market and meet the pace of capital.

Due to the rapid expansion of franchising and low replication costs, franchise companies have encouraged capital market to join in recent years. As the size of franchisors expand, more and more investment institutions are flooding into this field. Due to industry concerns, venture capital institutions have almost rushed into the franchise industry in the past two years. The participation of the capital market has optimised the franchise team, back-office construction, and more, and it has provided solid financial support for the expansion of direct stores. Of course, it will inevitably lead to mergers and acquisitions between brands. Although the injection of funds will support the development of franchising, franchisors will also face severe performance pressures and may even lead to rapid expansion losses. Therefore, there is still a lot of room for integration and discussion between the capital market and the franchise.

Today's franchise can take a look on the establishment of the space created by McDonald's, Holiday Inn, 21 Century, and others. From the beginning of trademark and product licensing to the rebirth of commercial forms, franchising is largely ubiquitous, and the degree of acceptance is increasing. An important point to remember is that the franchise provides the same value as it did today, tomorrow, and in the future. Regardless of its background or concept, and regardless of the size of the company, it is all in all a user-friendly business system. The question is not, "Should we do franchise?" The question is, "How can one or more forms of franchising help achieve expansion goals?" When a company tries to get close to the franchise, exciting events will follow.

Franchising has evolved into one of the most visible and open business forms in existence, and its emergence has created businesses with a few billion dollars in market capitalisation. Whether you are a world-renowned entrepreneur or an entrepreneur who watches TV at home and has many years of work experience, what makes you still hesitate?

Transform Your Own Brand to a New Trend

Become a world-wide Franchisor

When your brand is credible, unique, and teachable, you should seriously consider to open a franchise department to gain passive income! This business model will include franchisee trademarks, a complete set of marketing and management systems, including training, shop selection, code of conduct and financial system.

Franchising has been developed for more than 100 years and has developed tremendously in China and Hong Kong in recent years. It's time to fanchise!

To do that, you need

A Franchise Consultant!

If you have any concerns, I'm always acting as a franchise consultant, helping different franchisors to develop their own franchising systems. I have more than 10-years of franchising experience. On the path, you will never be alone as we will discuss the solutions together and face the transformation step by step in every stage to reach our target.

 Karen Kwan

 karenkwan1919@gmail.com

 kwan.karen

Karen Kwan

- Chairlady of Asia Branding & Franchising Association
- Chairlady of Early Childhood Organization Of Hong Kong
- General Secretary Of Business Lady Association
- Founder of Math Monkey (Hong Kong) Ltd.
- Event Director of Tak Ngai PR & Marketing Ltd.
- Certified Business Consultant by Blair Singer
- Licensed Practitioner of NLP
- Over 10 years experience in education and franchising

Join a Franchise Association in Asia in order to expose your brand in a target area.

ASIA BRANDING & FRANCHISING ASSOCIATION

Asia Branding & Franchising Association was established in 2014, and initially founded by a group of successful entrepreneurs who are keen to serve the community. We organize business events regularly such as seminars, workshops, tours, exhibitions, etc. and have a team of advisors from different professional aspects for our members. In 2017, we firstly introduced the 'Asia Branding and Franchising Award', assisting our members' brands to leap onto the world stage effectively.

JOIN US

www.abfa.asia
Tel: +852 2307 1091
Fax: +852 3011 6803
Whatsapp: +852 6999 7188
Email: enquiry@abfa.asia

To join ABFA Award
www.abfa-awards.com
Youtube: Asia Branding and Franchising Association

Hitting Your Target with Professional Systems

Tak Ngai PR and Marketing Limited is an event planning company in Hong Kong and a subsidiary of charity Tak Ngai Development Limted. We assists customers in planning and organizing large-scale events with innovative and effective methods. We provide both online and offline marketing strategies, aimings to expand the clients' business, and enable each customer to achieve brand promotion and brand building effectively!

Service Areas

Large-scale event
Tak Ngai will do everything for you to meet every aspect of the event, and achieve the goal of the event. So you can leave an incredible impression on the participants.

Conferences and seminars
Tak Ngai will make the most comprehensive planning and preparation for each of your meetings and seminars, conference sessions to ensure the overall outcome, and fluency!

Exhibition sales
Tak Ngai will help to promote your exhibition and help you to maximize the sales result of your brand!

Marketing and public relations
Tak Ngai promotes your brand to attract your target customers through creative and effective online and offline promotion.

+852 9699 3194
amyzee@takngai.asia
www.takngai.asia
+852 2307 1091

www.ingramcontent.com/pod-product-compliance
Lightning Source LLC
Chambersburg PA
CBHW030810180526
45163CB00003B/1223